THE QUEEN AND THE ARTS

Helen Cathcart

THE QUEEN AND THE ARTS

Published by Sapere Books.

20 Windermere Drive, Leeds, England, LS17 7UZ,
United Kingdom

saperebooks.com

ISBN: 978-1-80055-465-8.

TABLE OF CONTENTS

INTRODUCTION

The opening of the Queen's Gallery at Buckingham Palace in 1962 saw the spread of a new public awareness of the Queen's interest in the arts and caused fresh heed to be paid to the imaginative aspirations of the Royal Family. This was an explosive impact, for critics were alleging that the Royal Family had shown no interest in contemporary artistic development since the death of George IV, and their view was indeed negligently shared by many. The opening of the new Gallery moreover coincided with the final preparation of this book for press and the event seemed to heighten the need of disentangling the conflicting arguments.

At the outset, any close inquiry into the artistic interests of the Queen is fraught with the hazards of trespass into the inner realm of her private affairs. Though prompt and conscientious in assisting the author who seeks to interpret any public aspect of the monarchy, the appointed liaison officers of the Royal Household are here involved in a quandary, for it remains their vigilant and paramount task not to give private information, but to guard the confidences of the Queen with the utmost discretion.

This constant dilemma sharpens when the television cameras may observe the Queen on her visits to the racecourse, excursions that are becoming increasingly rare, and yet can seldom study and convey Her Majesty's enjoyment in music or painting. An undue emphasis upon royal open-air recreations has thus been frozen in print and we have read too little of quieter pleasures. The Englishman's noted love of sport, combined with his aesthetic diffidence, are alike the cause of our ill-founded opinion of the degree of royal responsibility towards the arts.

This book is intended for that daemon of my publisher's imagination, the average reader, rather than those already highly trained in professional art. Yet even the proficient may be tempted to draw inaccurate conclusions from the new protocol of reticence that not only shields the Queen but also inevitably swaddles and stifles our accurate knowledge of her as an individual.

Despite this impasse of public patronage and private taste, it will be obvious that I received both information and fruitful guidance in the preparation of this book, and for this I am most grateful. In the upshot the research on my theme was spread over two years. My inquiries led me from palace and castle to studios and exhibition galleries, from the library of the Royal Academy to such prime venues as the Royal College of Art, the Royal College of Music, the Royal Society of Arts, and the Arts Council.

Finally, I must express my special thanks to the secretaries of Buckingham Palace and Clarence House for the assistance they were able to give. Sir Anthony Blunt, Surveyor of the Queen's Pictures, was good enough to read and correct certain pages offered to his scrutiny; Mr. Humphrey Brooke, secretary of the Royal Academy of Arts, similarly read and revised the salient passages dealing with that institution, and I am particularly under obligation to Mr. Oliver Millar, Deputy Surveyor of the Queen's Pictures, for putting me right on other points of specific detail. This is not to say that approval was sought or gained at every turn, for this book could not have been written without considerable freedom of inquiry and interpretation. Last and not least, my thanks are also due to the artists and others who permitted me to trespass on their time, and

especially Mr. Alan Davie, Mr. Edward I. Halliday, Mr. John
Piper, Mr. Graham Sutherland, O. M., and Miss Anna
Zinkeisen.

London and Milland
1961–1963

1: THE CONTEMPORARY ROYAL COLLECTION

I

Every reign has its flavour, whether marked by a monarch's devotion to duty, his addiction to parental discipline or, more rarely, his pursuit of pleasure. Her Majesty Queen Elizabeth II is a monarch with an instinctive and sustaining sense of history. We may all recognize her innate qualities of dedication and self-discipline and her sovereign awareness of the vigour and continuity of tradition. One has but to study the Queen's life and work a little closer to discover that her sincerity of purpose is strengthened by a breadth of vision wider than is generally realized, and that with the Queen's inflexible personal standards there is linked a highly resilient, youthful and receptive response to new ideas.

At the threshold of this decade of the sixties a movement was afoot to celebrate the tercentenary of the Restoration of the Monarchy, but the Queen demurred. Plans were blithely discussed in the Press, questions were set down in Parliament, controversy arose on whether it would be better to commemorate the landing of Charles II as King at Kingston on Spey or whether the true anniversary related to his ceremonious arrival at Dover. Yet we may infer that the Prime Minister was speaking with the Queen's agreement and perhaps her prompting when he declined the proposed festivities and remarked that it would be better "to concentrate on the present" and that an opening of Parliament or the birth of a royal infant were more suitable for celebration than "a particular incident from the past".

This was the winter of content when the Queen awaited the advent of Prince Andrew, and the reprieve from many duties brought a phase of unaccustomed freedom and relaxation, a time, indeed, for reflection and for luxuriating in the domestic joys. The Queen liked to walk in the afternoon in the Palace grounds, but in inclement weather she often strolled in the Palace itself; and if one objective beckoned more than another, the private Picture Gallery has always been a favourite retreat.

When the rain is drumming upon the glass roof, when concealed lighting warms the murky February daylight and a fire is lit in one of the hearths, the old Gallery has a cosy and welcoming air of sanctuary. Here, in a place of honour, is Rembrandt's youthful portrait of himself and Saskia in their marriage year; here also his dusky and mysterious *Adoration of the Magi*, and his renowned *The Shipbuilder and His Wife*. Here, too, is the scene of *St. George and the Dragon*, which Charles I commissioned when Rubens was staying in England as Netherlands ambassador, a picture showing the King cast in the role of the rescuing knight and his consort as the benighted Princess on the banks of a Thames that never was. And here usually, when not on loan or public view, is George III's Vermeer, *The Music Lesson*, long hung at Windsor Castle, but brought to Buckingham Palace some thirty years ago because Queen Mary wished it to be seen more often by her guests.

The Queen has known these pictures from childhood and is as familiar with their histories as if they were relatives involved in family anecdote. The Rubens *St. George* is one of the great original pictures of Charles I's collection, sold perhaps for £150 by Cromwell and surviving many vicissitudes in the hands of Cardinal Richelieu and the Duc d'Orleans before being returned to the British Crown under George IV. The Vermeer was purchased by mistake just two centuries ago when Vermeer was little known and his signature was misread as "Van Meiris". Rembrandt's *Shipbuilder* was bought at Christie's at a time when viewers reverentially doffed their hats on approaching a masterpiece... The Van Dyck portraits and Titian landscapes, the Hobbemas and Frans Hals, all have their stories, and the paintings in the private Palace gallery are, of course, barely a cross-section, a few stars in the splendid galaxy of the Royal Collection, totalling five thousand works and more. Yet the Queen is on terms "far better than acquaintance with the greater proportion", to quote the words of a member of her staff. Enjoying her pictures year after year, becoming increasingly familiar with every nuance and detail of a painting, there are many Her Majesty regards with true affection and, conscientious in everything, she feels a constant obligation of stewardship for them all.

The perspective of events, however, sufficiently displays the special claim that the royal art treasures gained on the Queen's thoughts as she awaited her third child. The proposals for celebrating the tercentenary of the restored monarchy did not entirely fall on stony ground. The Queen eagerly welcomed her Royal Academy's decision to mark the event by devoting an exhibition to the Age of Charles II, and no fewer than forty-nine royal pictures and pieces of furnishing were lent to that memorable reassembly of the English renaissance. Less exacting than any other medium, Her Majesty's personal emotional attitude to the Restoration could be better distilled through the fine arts.

The tragic fate of Charles I was matched by the dispersal of his art collection, which, the verdict of history assures us, had been ranked among the finest in the world. The King's pictures included "Titians without a rival", and "Correggios unsurpassed", and the Puritan Commonwealth hastily sold

Tintorettos at £100 apiece, Holbeins at £50, and a priceless Rubens self-portrait was lumped in disgrace with other pictures. Multiplied by twelve to twenty times for today's values, the bargains explain the frantic gold rush that ensued on the part of every picture dealer and civilized collector in Europe. At the Restoration, eleven years later, most of the pictures that had crossed the Channel were scattered irretrievably. Eight of the Titians are still in the Louvre, Raphael's *La Perla* and Andrea del Sarto's *Holy Family* rest in the Prado, Raphael's *St. George* remains oddly exiled in Leningrad. When Charles II came to the throne only the poorer remnants of his father's great gallery could be reclaimed from English collectors. Many paintings had been made over to Civil Servants of the republic in lieu of salaries; a few had been valued and catalogued for sale before being rescued and stored in perilous hiding in attics and cellars, and the odyssey of recovery has been in progress ever since. Queen Mary was instrumental in restoring the Elsheimer *St. Christopher* and an early portrait of Charles I by Mytens was returned to the Queen by legacy in 1961.

To the Queen, as I have said, these are oft-told and familiar stories, episodes steeped in family atmosphere, part of the perennial context of her everyday life. When the Queen lent so many of her Charles II treasures to Burlington House she was herself, in fact, celebrating the inspiring burst of artistic ideas that came with Charles and his Court from abroad, and the renewal of artistic Court patronage that saw the beginning of a native English school of art. Apart from the intimate, personal enjoyment of her pictures, there is no doubt that, in a scholarly sense, the Queen sees her collection steadily and sees it in wholesome historical context. The fifty years that followed the era of Charles II found little added to the royal collection other than the Kneller portraits. When George II's consort, Queen Caroline, inquisitively examined a neglected bureau at Kensington Palace and found a lost book of Holbein drawings, together with an album of Leonardos, she chanced to inaugurate a century of renewed attention to the arts. The atmosphere of the late Georgian age may have stemmed more directly from the Throne than we commonly imagine. "The King and Lord Bute have certainly both of them great propensity to the arts," wrote Horace Walpole. George III commissioned his Gainsboroughs direct from the artist, richly patronized Zoffany and other portraitists and enriched Windsor with a collection of Dutch, Flemish and Italian paintings, among them an array of fifty-three Canalettos.

Both as Regent and King, George IV was not only a magnificent patron of the contemporary artists of his day, but he acquired such a passion for Dutch paintings that his eager and extravagant saleroom prices were unsurpassed for sixty years. To George IV, also, the royal collection owes some of its finest Rubens and Van Dycks, for as fast as these wanderers of the Charles I collection came on the market the King snapped them up and brought them home.

Queen Victoria and the Prince Consort, too, were not enslaved solely to the sentiment — or the cunning skill — of Winterhalter, Landseer, and Frith. Though swindled on occasion, the Prince Consort ardently collected Italian primitives and acquired the *Duccio Triptych*, a Fra Angelico, and the Gentile de Fabriano *Madonna*. Queen Victoria, though sadly ignoring the mainstream of English watercolour painters, amassed at least a characteristic collection in this vein of scenes of pomp and pageantry.

As for Edward VII, he was not the vulgarian that has sometimes been depicted. "I do not know much about Arrt," he would say, with the guttural rolling of his r's, "but I think I know something about Arr-r-angement." It was he who first sponsored the magnificent series of catalogues and portfolio books on the royal art collections which have continued to the present time, and now include an abstruse study of Castiglione and volumes on the Venetian and Bolognese drawings at Windsor that our own Queen has herself offered as gifts to relatives and friends.

We have the unexpected testimony of Sir Owen Morshead that King George V was similarly "much attached" to his pictures, while Queen Mary's celebrated preoccupation with filling historic gaps in the Collection established an interest that Queen Elizabeth II still notably sustains. King George VI had all too little time for fostering the arts in his brief and war-torn reign. Yet he was primarily responsible in 1946 for furthering the Royal Academy's winter "Exhibition of the King's Pictures", perhaps the greatest public display of royal paintings ever seen, and it has been suggested that the idea of turning part of the bombed private chapel at the Palace into a picture gallery was originally his.

From Charles I to our own day, such then was the panorama of royal patronage that undoubtedly influenced the Queen early in 1960 when she declined to commemorate the "incident" of the restoration of the monarchy and yet wished to make a palpable gesture of artistic patronage as a thank-offering joined in a closer sense with the natal festivities of Prince Andrew. As a Court official explained it to me, rather without conviction, "The Queen felt it incumbent on her to continue the tradition of the royal collection." But it is clear that Her Majesty knew precisely what she wished to do and how she wished to do it. Nearly all her predecessors had made a contribution highly characteristic of their time. Each and every monarch had hall-marked the additions of his or her reign with the idiosyncrasies of personal taste. The Queen and the Duke of Edinburgh were even then supervising the remodelling in distinctive contemporary style of a set of private apartments at Windsor Castle which, within the limitations of their historic frame, were being redecorated to afford the simplicity, comfort, and untrammelled light and space characteristic of the interior décor of our time. As a finishing touch, the Queen decided, the fresh walls should be graced and enlivened by a number of paintings by living British artists and the paintings should be her personal choice of current work.

In March, 1960, the Queen so commanded, and she asked that a number of paintings should be assembled for her selection, stipulating only that they should be contemporary in the actual sense of being representative of the moment. Her implied preference was for the artists of her own generation who were coming into view, and initially no painters were specified by name. It scarcely mattered if the artists were renowned or obscure, *avant-garde* or steeped in tradition. A royal net was to scoop a comprehensive sample from the cross-currents of contemporary British art, and from this sampling the Queen was to make a more confined private selection that would be entirely individual and completely her own.

II

The mechanics of the royal choice may be of interest. As many as five thousand new paintings are estimated to be on view in London at a given time and from these the Queen wished to take not the cream but a small yet representative cross-sample of excellence. The number of paintings to be chosen was limited to ten or a dozen by the available wall space at

Windsor, while the scope and style of the works was narrowed only by the knowledge of the Queen's preferences formed by the aides appointed to gather the preliminary selection of paintings for her to see. Even so, some unlikely submissions were included, as it was proper they should be, and two gained the Queen's final approval against all expectations.

Three of the younger members of the royal staff — Sir Martin Charteris as an assistant private secretary, Lord Plunket as an official noted for his discriminating interest in the fine arts, and Mr. William Heseltine as a young Commonwealth attaché — performed their commission under the supervision of Sir Anthony Blunt, Surveyor of the Queen's Pictures.

For a few weeks in the early spring the trio moved through artistic London like agents of Haroun-al-Raschid. All the one-man exhibitions were visited, and Keith Vaughan, Alan Davie, Francis Bacon, and Denis Wirth-Miller may be noted among the artists who at that time had qualifying work on show. As Professor of History of Art at London University, Sir Anthony Blunt was in natural sympathy with graduates of the Slade, but noticeably "leaned over backward" to be fair to the rival claims of the Royal College of Art. The Royal Academy, the Courtauld Institute and other bodies were consulted in the cause of including artists of merit whose names perhaps eluded the recommendations of private dealers. No time was wasted, however, in meeting the Queen's wishes. Over a hundred works were rapidly assembled at Buckingham Palace and from these the Queen selected a score or so to be sent to Windsor Castle for a closer judgment in their intended permanent setting.

No art consultants and indeed no members of the Household were present when the Queen and Prince Philip made their ultimate choice one Saturday afternoon. The Queen desired even then to be emphatically sure of her decision and a dozen works were deferred for approval the following weekend. The plan to buy ten pictures was, in fact, amplified by the decision to include one of Barbara Hepworth's drawings of the operating theatre, her *Arthrodesis of the Hip*, which summarizes the delicacy and precision of this series with extraordinary tension. If it may be obvious that this struck a deep chord of compassion in the Queen, it is equally notable as the only one of the chosen works to contain a human figure. There is also only one still life in the highly characteristic *Flower Piece* by Mary Fedden, a grouping of bouquets swaddled in cellophane with some evocation of huddled waste that must have struck the same mainsprings of intense personal emotion. This painting was acquired direct from the artist.

Seven of the paintings are landscapes, widely different in genre, but all have a curious quality in common. All are singularly free of human figures and activity, blandly evoking empty, expansive spaces in an almost empty world. It may occur to some that *Castle Howard* by Robin Darwin and *Les Toits* by James Taylor are complementary. The *Castle*, with its Vanbrugh domes and pediments, festive fountains and muted opulence, is in sympathy, we can imagine, with regal reminiscence. *Les Toits*, the old rooftops jumbled in grey and red beneath a sombre sky, is the veritable backdrop the Queen must have seen above the crowds in a hundred spruced-up cities, perhaps recapitulating the essence of royal travel better than forests of bunting above massed pavements. James Taylor, who lived in Paris, seldom courting publicity, was one of the younger artists of the selection, barely 35 when his picture was purchased. Yet the choice was perceptive: this painting already contains the authority and precision of his subsequent large canvas *Spanish Landscape*, for which his earlier roof perspective now seems but a rehearsal piece. Again, Robin Darwin's *Castle Howard* has been considered the least modern painting of the group, or alternatively the painting best rooted in tradition, and the cap may fit Mr. Darwin as Principal of the Royal College of Art. It is said that the Queen on seeing the picture immediately recognized his eloquent style and at once remarked: "That's by Mr. Darwin." Darwin had, however, been photographed at his easel by his students, this very painting visibly mounted before him, and the photograph may have been seen by the Queen in the weekly magazine in which it was published. Royal memories are notoriously retentive, and even a queen may court the apt remark on occasion.

Since Mary Fedden was similarly a Royal College tutor, it must be said that Roger de Grey as another tutor of the painting school assisted in a notable hat-trick for the College when the Queen also chose one of his landscapes. The idiosyncrasy of applying his pastel colour in a series of "slats" was a technique the artist made recognizably his own, and here again his *March Landscape* is a scene of tender personal evocation for the Queen, perhaps of the bleak beauty of a late winter day in the Sandringham coverts. If King George V once remarked, "I know what I like", one can accept that his granddaughter likes what she knows. The Queen's choice of another painting within this context, *Suffolk Landscape* by Kenneth Rowntree, also saw this artist, once a student of the Slade and formerly on the staff of the Royal College of Art, accorded the notable honour of being the only painter with more than one work in this major contemporary purchase. (His *Putney Boats* reduces to elemental forms a placid becalmed dignity blended with humour which the Queen could not resist.) This approval of two pictures was a mark of merit in turn to the Leicester Galleries, through whom both paintings had been submitted, and it was to prove a third triumph for their sponsorship when the Queen also decided to buy a third painting they had tendered, *Firwood Ride* by Ivon Hitchens.

This work continues Hitchens's thirteen variations on his firwood ride theme, autumnal, wintry, and in spring, which he had shown the previous year, but now his simplified, almost abstract forms were carried to the verdant tunnel of high summer. Nearing his sixties, Ivon Hitchens was the senior artist in the Queen's selection, yet the choice fell appropriately on one who has been called one of the most uncompromising and representive *English* painters. A veteran of eighteen one-man shows, an exhibitor in five continents, a product of the St. John's Wood and Royal Academy schools, his works have been acquired by the Tate Gallery, the Victoria and Albert Museum, the Arts Council, the British Council, a dozen provincial galleries and as many more overseas. In contrast, one may now mention Wirth-Miller, distinctive in being self-taught, who had held his first one-man exhibition with great success at the Lefevre Gallery only the month before his *Landscape* was sent down to Windsor. It could not have been better essayed if deliberately designed for the Queen, which was, of course, far from the case. Here was another painting with the full lyricism of the Suffolk school, and here also a young artist of strange and undisputed talent who received the immeasurable benefice of royal patronage at the very onset of his career.

The seventh of the landscape artists, however, received the cachet of the Queen's interest after already winning the warm accord of world-wide recognition as one of Australia's foremost artists. Sidney Nolan's tawny *Australian Landscape* is set in date between his "Masked Man" and "Leda and the Swan" periods. Submitted by the Matthiesen Gallery, his landscape is a harsh and savage concept, representational yet comfortless and inimical. With its barbaric cacti and sullen rocks, this is an Australia the Queen could scarcely have glimpsed on her travels, and its inclusion preserves royal taste from any charge of sentimentality. Save for the choice of Nolan, the Queen's selection would have been limited to artists of the British Isles. Nolan, however, joined Rubery Bennett, Bryan Mansell, Jean Ramsay, Albert Namatjira, and William Dobell among the paintings of Australian artists acquired for the royal collection in the present reign.

So one turns finally and sharply to the eleventh in the Windsor grouping of contemporary pictures, as if to a clear exposition that the Queen's taste is neither fettered by convention nor yet timid of adherence to a younger vogue. *Throne of the Eye Goddess* by Alan Davie (referred to as *Untitled No. 19* at the time of the Queen's purchase) is a vehemently organized abstract readily recognizable to anyone in the least acquainted with the expressionist imagery and meteoric rise of this gifted and defiant Scottish painter. One critic has praised him for some of the most spectacular and exciting paintings seen in twenty years; while the same protagonist in the same breath has denounced some of his compositions as trivial. Alan Davie won the Guthrie Award of the Royal Scottish Academy, when he was 20 years old, for the best painting of the year by a young artist. Simultaneously he began to desert his highly gifted naturalism in his first attempts in expressionism, and he has acknowledged Paul Klee, Picasso, Jackson Pollock, and Rothko among his earlier influences. He held his first one-man show in an Edinburgh bookshop in 1946, was encouraged by the Gimpel Brothers for his first one-man show in their London Gallery in 1950, and was rarely absent from any appropriate group exhibition of modern painting. His work has been acquired by public collections as various as the Tate, the

Museum of Modern Art in New York, the Stedelijk in Amsterdam, and the Albright in Buffalo. It seems probable that the Queen knew of his work as early as 1956, when it was already being exhibited abroad by the British Council. It must be remembered, too, that in selecting a Davie for her private rooms the Queen acted without the restraints of public observation. Her purchases were private. The paintings would be seen, it was thought, only by her closest friends.

Ivon Hitchens, Robin Darwin, Barbara Hepworth, Mary Fedden, Kenneth Rowntree, Roger de Grey, Denis Wirth-Miller, Sidney Nolan, James Taylor, and Alan Davie, fashionables and unfashionables, mature and youthful, the artists grouped in the Queen's selection already form a generous unity. The Royal Academy, the Royal Scottish Academy, the Royal College of Arts, the Slade and the Ruskin School, all have satisfaction in the laurels shared among former pupils. The Lefevre, the Matthiesen, the Leicester Galleries, and Gimpel Fils were among the dealers' salons to implement distinction in pleasing the Queen. It was once pleaded, long, long ago, that the annual meanderings of the aristocracy were good for trade. It must be equally good for an artist to be represented at Windsor Castle, as if they had been awarded an endowment assurance of the recognition of posterity.

The Queen's purchase of 1960 was not her first and it has not been her latest, but it ranks nevertheless as one of the largest and most liberal instances of the royal patronage of contemporary art for many years. To trace an equal precedent, we have to return through six reigns to the lavish expenditures of George IV, with his direct purchases from Reynolds, Lawrence, Hoppner, Wilkie, Haydon, and his cashbook entries, "£124.10.6d to the widow of Gainsborough". But art since then has spread its wings, and it might be said justly that if the modern purchases of 1960 were the sum total, if this were all, it would not be enough. Happily, it is a demonstrable fact that the present Royal Family's beneficence to art had already developed in the first decade of the Queen's reign more liberally than through the reigns of a century past. The Duke of Edinburgh, for example, enjoyed pricking balloons at the expense of extremists, as many of us do: "Who perpetrated this?" he would cry, or "Look what they're asking for it!" His quips did not prevent him from commissioning two further paintings for Windsor from William Dobell, known for a decade as one of Australia's most extreme and controversial painters. Moreover, Prince Philip went out of his way to ask Dobell to paint whatever he liked. This, surely, is the modern match of George IV crying, "Let Wilkie choose the subject, take his time and fix his own price." In particular, Dobell achieved a measure of notoriety for his distorted and masochistic portraits. In 1943, when he won Australia's premier art award, the Archibald Prize, for a portrait, two competing artists challenged the decision, contending that his work was caricature, not a portrait, and a lawsuit followed. The Duke of Edinburgh ignored the restraints that might have been provoked by this storm scene; the commissioned paintings, it was thought, would be a landscape and a figure work. But in the event, in 1961, Dobell contributed two scenic pieces to Windsor, one depicting a surf carnival, the other no less Australian and even Hogarthian in the lively atmosphere of a country race meeting.

Although we are primarily concerned with the artistic preoccupations of the Queen, one cannot in practice readily sift the shared common interests of husband and wife. Prince Philip seldom paid an official visit to an art exhibition without selecting and subsequently buying at least one picture, often, one may assume, a work judged to appeal to his wife. The Queen on occasion has similarly purchased paintings by Edward Seago, no doubt because his firm and dramatic landscapes particularly appealed to her husband. If a purple seal were significantly allowed to replace the customary red label for a "sold" picture, we could perceive how regularly and discriminately royal purchases are made at the Royal Academy summer exhibition and in other salons year after year.

Many of these pictures are probably used to give pleasure in the private sphere of gifts, and thus gain no permanent foothold in the royal collections. Yet the Queen has often bought or commissioned pictures with deeper purpose, for she evidences that she appreciates the emollient power of art in international diplomacy, and she has, in fact, restored the fine arts to one of their old ceremonial functions as matters of gift between heads of State on State occasions.

Thus, when visiting Coventry to lay the foundation stone of the new Cathedral in March, 1956, Her Majesty was shown the replicas of Graham Sutherland's cartoons for his immense tapestry of *Christ in Glory in the Tetramorph*, and this experience was to have an immediate sequel. No one can look on this great endeavour with the sensibilities unstirred, but, in particular, the heraldic qualities of the four Beasts caged in their cubes around the central figure and mobile against their varied, peculiarly contemporary backgrounds of purple, grey, pale blue and brown most evidently impressed the Queen. Shortly afterwards, in Menton, Graham Sutherland received a letter asking whether he would undertake to paint a composition on behalf of the Queen and the Duke of Edinburgh for presentation to the President of Portugal on the occasion of their State Visit in 1957. The work was to symbolize the common interests in history of Portugal and

England and, having regard to the bats, snakes, toads and sinister creatures prolific in Sutherland's work at this time, the commission clearly required firm courage from its patrons. Fortunately, the artist revelled in the compulsion of again working under pressure on a neo-romantic composition of twisting tendrils and exotic forms in the mood in which his creative activities can equally luxuriate, and two finished paintings were submitted. Her Majesty bought the pair and one was owned by Prince Philip.

From another sphere of artistic composition, with similar intention came the collage of fabric and needlework which the Queen bought from the designer, Miss Margaret Kaye, and gave to the people of Ghana on the occasion of her visit in 1961, for use as an altar frontal in Accra Cathedral.

This serves us as an instance of royal patronage, of the special commerce behind sovereign and artist, in its most direct and time-honoured form. A student under Miss Kaye at the Camberwell Art School worked with extra impetus, so he told me, at the thought that he, too, might one day win royal recognition. Such gifts are mentioned too seldom in official schedules and announcements, though the commission bestows special recognition upon the established and distributes firmer benefits in commissions and cash to the young. But why the reticence? In 1958 it was quietly announced that the Duke of Edinburgh had bought some paintings while visiting the Royal Scottish Academy summer exhibition. In reality, it turned out that he had purchased fourteen works, and had since purchased at least another twenty-one.

The first selection ranged from a characteristic landscape by Ian Fleming, R.S.A., to a still life by Marjorie Stark, under the prosaic kitchen-sink label *Hake in Enamel Dish*. The total 1958 purchase included works by Robin Philipson and Ernest Dinkel, Edmund Blampied, Murray Thomson, Margery Clinton, and William Birnie. There were still lifes by Alexander Goudie, James Cumming, and Carole Gibbons. Tom Hutcheson contributed a study of the Lanarkshire slag heaps, and the Duke admired the vigorous inspiration Druie Bowett had derived from the Renishaw Iron Works. Some of these names are still unfamiliar in England. Scottish art still draws its vigorous strength from tradition and relies to an exceptional degree on purely regional custom and appreciation. In keeping with this local spirit, all the pictures have been fittingly honoured by being hung in the palace of Holyroodhouse, where they serve a highly practical purpose in helping to enliven the dour private apartments.

It can be added that this royal gesture, with its repeated encouragement and influence, had not cost a great deal. Edmund Blampied's study of horses, priced at ninety guineas, was Prince Philip's most expensive purchase and may have been considered the picture most likely to appeal to the Queen. The entire first selection, with the catalogued prices, was as follows:

Cock and Hen: Robin Philipson
Hake in Enamel Dish: Marjorie Stark (£16)
Flower Piece and Paraqueet: Ernest Dinkel (£45)
Horses: Edmund Blampied (£94.10s.)
November: E. M. Murray Thomson (£21)
Shipyard in Kent: Anne Finlay (£26.5s.)
Winter's Moon: Ian Fleming (£40)
Still Life in Blue: Alexander Goudie (£25)
Frosty Morning, Kilbarchen: William Birnie (£12.12s.)
Fairfield's Yard: Margery Clinton (£15)
Still Life by the Door: James W. H. Cumming (£40)
Slag Formations, Lanarkshire: Tom Hutcheson (£35)

Still Life: Carole Gibbons
Renishaw Iron Works: Druie Bowett (£21)

The expenditure, though lavish, thus totalled approximately, only £500. We should remember that this sum, however, represented no small percentage of Prince Philip's net personal income. We are far from the days when the Prince Regent felt he could afford to pay £9,000 for six Dutch pictures, and Scottish artists could scarcely have expected Prince Philip to repeat his demonstration of interest and goodwill for a number of years. Nevertheless, in June, 1961, when the Duke again spent a morning at the Royal Scottish Academy with the Queen, he purchased another six paintings. As if with special care in selection, none of the artists previously honoured had their work chosen on this occasion. The full list comprised:

Flower with Orange Background: Mary Armour (£57.15s.)
Sea Tangle: Guy Worsdell (£36.15s.)
Night Fish: J. D. Robertson (£50)
Winter Landscape: Shearer Armstrong (£31.10s.)
Flowers and White Dish: David McClure (£50)
Rosemarkie: W. Drummond Bone (£40)

These paintings possibly bear the impress of the Queen's approval more than the works singled out by her husband alone. Perhaps, so compatible were the sympathies of husband and wife, we may regard this as a joint purchase, although it was completed in Prince Philip's name. In 1962, moreover, the Duke also bought *Still Life with Black Lace* by Mary Armour and a riverside scene, *Torry Grey*, by Ian Fleming, thus doubly emphasizing that an artist already represented at Holyroodhouse was not disqualified from a second contribution. Another artist, Ronald Watson, indeed had the distinction of two pictures in the Duke's 1962 selection. It is also of interest that three of the 1962 pictures — all black-and-white drawings — were quickly chosen on the spot, and twelve paintings were ordered the following day after the Duke had studied the catalogue. The highest price was £75, the total reached £518.7s. The complete 1962 list purchase was:

> *Still Life with Black Lace*: Mary Armour (£75)
> *View of Back Gardens*: Gordon S. Cameron (£75)
> *Torry Grey*: Ian Fleming (£50)
> *White Owl over Cornfield*: Shand Hutchison (£50)
> *Still Life with Polyanthus*: William Armour (£40)
> *Rock Mynydd Bodafon*: Donald McIntyre (£40)
> *Winter, Mill Brow*: Judith da Fano (£31.10s.)
> *Green Day*: Irene Halliday (£30)
> *West Wemyss*: David Ewans (£25)
> *Longforgan Halt*: Ellen Malcolm (£25)
> *Schoolhouse Garden*: Frances Walker (£25)
> *Cold Day*: Cecile E. M. Johnston (£15.15s.)
> *Beneath the Bridge* (Drawing): Ian J. Massie (£12.12s.)
> *Demolition* (Drawing): Ronald Watson (£12)
> *Dusk* (Drawing): Ronald Watson (£12)

We have already evidenced that in the first decade of the reign the Queen and her husband bought more contemporary paintings of quality than any monarch for longer than a century past. We have attended the purchase of upwards of fifty paintings and shall have occasion to hear of many more. Is this the neglect of the arts of which high-minded critics carp … or is it the flowering of an eager and stimulating interest? We must now define the challenge and explore beyond the lip-service of patronage. It may not be unrewarding to trace the Queen's taste and enthusiasm to its mainsprings and so follow the broad current of modern royal appreciation from its source.

2: "A CULTIVATED APPRECIATION"

I

In studying the artistic influences around the Queen we need to return in imagination not to the solitude of an only child but to the girlhood of a Princess whose character was early tempered by more than four years seniority to her sister. Reflective by nature, the Queen, as Princess Elizabeth, became schooled in the capacity to amuse herself. Her mother taught her to read when she was five years old; books and pictures became her everyday companions, and later there came the fructifying responsibility of reading books and explaining pictures to Princess Margaret. Although Princess Elizabeth was only six when Miss Marion Crawford arrived on the scene, the governess could early detect her pupil's high I.Q. and wonderful memory, her amenable and sensitive quickness of mind. Academic standards were never the first requirement of the royal curriculum. The Duchess of York, the late Queen Mother, desired her children to acquire good manners and deportment and above all, we are told, she wished them to acquire a cultivated appreciation of the arts.

This is characteristic. A considerable proportion of the public service of the young Duchess of York's early married life had been particularly devoted to the arts. She was indefatigable in visiting exhibition galleries and attending concerts, inaugurating displays of embroidery and antiques, inspecting murals and sculptures and handicrafts. So far as a royal lady can, she had gone out of her way to make the arts her *métier*.

One of the first public affairs to which she ever took her elder daughter was, significantly, a concert at the old Queen's Hall. One of her first impromptu royal speeches was as patron of the Royal Academy of Dramatic Art, and, among the listening students, Griffith Jones remembered her "light, silvery voice" years later. Painters as fundamentally diverse as Matthew Smith and Ben Nicholson experienced the benefit of the Duchess of York's warm interest. There may be a period tang now to a description of her home at 145 Piccadilly with the Edmund Brock portrait of Princess Elizabeth over the mantelpiece, the "fine bronzes" that stood among the mass of exquisitely arranged flowers. But on the walls were the works of Sisley, Sickert, and Wilson Steer, painters undoubtedly as representative of their time as the Queen's own contemporary choice today.

Art is, of course, not the whole story: the Duchess of York also wished her children to spend as much time as possible in the open air, and riding and country pursuits had due attention. But if the young Princess listened to her elders gossiping of horses and gardens, conversational topics were equally devoted to books and music and pictures. At St. Paul's Walden Bury, where as a little girl Princess Elizabeth often spent summer weeks with her maternal grandmother, Lady Strathmore, the nursery wing still had the Marcus Stone and other storybook pictures which had been framed and hung by a gardener when her mother was small. Then, beyond a green baize door, was the grown-up world, a Georgian house of deep serenity and beauty with its pictures few but enriching: a Gainsborough in the entry hall, a Van Dyck, a Bellini and other Venetian and Florentine paintings. In the little library, on a rainy day, the Princess was no doubt permitted to look through the albums of flower paintings collected by an earlier Countess of

Strathmore, Mary Eleanor, when the house was new. On sunny days, in the garden, the John Nost statuary — the Hercules, the Wrestlers, the Running Footman and the rest — enjoyed rightful prominence. At 145 Piccadilly and Royal Lodge, Windsor, apart from the "Subjects" fitted into the schoolroom curriculum of writing and composition, poetry, music, singing and drawing, at least an hour each day was devoted to reading as part of a planned conquest of the juvenile foothills of literature. Against each changing scene of the royal year the petals of sensibility were gently encouraged to unfold in a civilized atmosphere of culture and refinement.

At Sandringham, King George V liked his granddaughter's company on the after-lunch trudge round the stables, but at Buckingham Palace he would set aside his papers and equally enjoy taking his "sweet little Lilibet" on a tour of the pictures in his private rooms. Here was Frith's *Ramsgate Sands* with all its lively byplay and crowded figures, paddlers and picnic parties and sand-pie makers, for the King to expound. Here, too, was Meissonier's *La Rixe* with its struggling antagonists in their fury of crimson, white and brown. Sir Owen Morshead has testified, as we have seen, that the King was "much attached" to his pictures. The elderly man could unbend to meet the nine-year-old girl on the common ground of imagination. He might pass over Reynolds's *Death of Dido* or the Delaroche portraits of Napoleon, but could build a lively jovial tale around Mulready's *Wolf and the Lamb*. The quarrelling schoolboys, with lifelike fidelity in every brush-stroke, precisely told the story that the King and indeed the child expected from pictures. The two Landseers, *Quiz, the Lion Dog* and *Dash, Nero and Lorey*, though of peculiar breed, were fond favourites. But King George V also admired the Winterhalters he kept near his view, particularly the *Florinda* group, a birthday gift from Queen Victoria to Prince Albert.

Then there were the crowded Wilkies, *The Penny Wedding*, with its Scottish guests, each of whom had obviously contributed their penny to the wedding feast, and the *Maid of Saragossa*, a lady of intrepid action manning a gun and giving epic attention to a carrier pigeon when all around her lay killed. We cannot resist a smile at these Victorian and pre-Victorian flavours, but the King was a man of secret sentiment, indulgent in conveying his warm enjoyment to his granddaughter. He was also fond of his Hoppners and kept them close to hand — or, rather, under his affectionate eye — in his private rooms. *The Comic Muse*, a portrait of Mrs. Jordan, was brought in from a staircase landing, because the King wished to see it more often.

There were also the Tuxen coronation groups and a huge canvas of the ceremony by John Bacon. The King enjoyed pointing out familiar family figures to his audience. He was proud of showing an attractive Cope portrait of his own father, King Edward VII, in evening dress. "The only good one I've got of him," he would gruffly remark. He said little of the sombre Luke Fildes portrait of Queen Alexandra in mourning for her eldest son, the King's brother, past which visitors were invariably ushered without comment, although the picture always continued to hang prominently in his private suite. "Occasion paintings", from christenings to public ceremonies, were also crowded together where space availed, each new event increasing the clutter. King George V managed to dispose of one of Lord Leighton's huge half-clad classic processionals by lending it to Edinburgh and then replaced it with a populous and uniformed scene by Frank Salisbury. But such substitutions were rare.

These paintings around King George and Queen Mary were thus, apart from the pictures in her own parents' home, the first to become familiar to our present Queen. She listened attentively when her grandfather told her his anecdotes, and years later, as it turned out, was able to recount them afresh to guests of her own. A member of General de Gaulle's visiting suite admired a sketch of a French soldier swaggering in scarlet uniform. The Queen told him it had been called "one of Granny's bargains". While being shown round the studio of the artist, Detaille, in Paris, Queen Mary had escaped the blandishments of the major works on his walls, but had then spotted the little sketch in a drawer and borne it off in triumph. Economy was vindicated and no doubt Queen Mary was right...

II

A wider formative step in our present Queen's artistic outlook occurred when her father succeeded as King George VI and the family went to live in Buckingham Palace. Although the exploration of the Palace was not as rapid as has been supposed, a whole new world gradually unfolded to the then Princess, with her retentive mind and observant eyes. A nodding acquaintance, destined to deepen to firm affection, was made with the pensive Gainsborough ladies and with the royal children of a past age who gazed from their Zoffany portraits, the boys in elegant suits of lilac and crimson, the princesses with their baskets of flowers. From Teniers's *A Village Dance* to the De Hooch *Game of Cards*, the Picture Gallery itself offered much for junior admiration. The smallest picture in the royal collection, *A Maidservant Cleaning a Pan* by Gerard Dou, barely six inches square, is said to have aroused instincts of special intimacy and protection, and if the young

33

Princess came to regard this little treasure as peculiarly her own, several other typical Dou pictures availed to lead her to fresh knowledge and comparison. Quickly grasping the wonderful educational possibilities that lay to hand, her governess, Miss Crawford, asked permission for one picture each week to be brought to the Palace schoolroom so that the children might study it at leisure and get to know it.

Probably the larger paintings were barred from this hospitality, but there were sufficient Dutch and Flemish pictures for ample variety and even a disputed Titian may have briefly found its way to the schoolroom while more worldly scholars argued its precise origins. No list appears to have been kept of the works surveyed in this way, but the children greeted each painting with fresh interest and delight — except on one occasion. The picture studies were resumed after the summer holiday at Balmoral and it was discovered that, after a surfeit of Landseers, the selected picture of the week mounted and awaiting them in the schoolroom was Landseer's *Dignity and Impudence*.

At the early age of eleven Princess Elizabeth had thus already been trained to look at paintings with an insight and knowledge rare in a child. A good example of the skill she had gained in remembering and making comparison arose shortly before her father's Coronation when she was taken with her sister to see the famous gilded State coach that has been a glory of Coronation processions since King George III. Seven-year-old Princess Margaret bounced happily up and down on the red cushions, but Princess Elizabeth more studiously examined the painted allegorical panels by Cipriani — Mars, Minerva and Mercury supporting the Imperial Crown and the rest. "Where have I seen these before?" she asked. "I feel sure I have seen some like them." Miss Crawford hazarded the Verrio ceilings at Windsor and the similar William Kent ceilings at Kensington Palace, but the Princess was unsatisfied. There are, in fact, four very similar Cipriani paintings embodied in the drawing-room ceiling at Broadlands, and Princess Elizabeth had seen them when visiting the Mountbatten home with her parents a few weeks earlier.

Queen Mary also now took an increasing interest in her granddaughter's education, taking her on afternoon visits to the National Gallery, the British Museum, the Kensington museums and the Wallace collection. Remembering how her own elderly Aunt Augusta had tutored her youthful artistic discrimination and fired her passion for collecting, Queen Mary was anxious to pass on the torch of these enthusiasms to her granddaughter.

Here, too, Princess Elizabeth came under a beneficial influence that enabled her to see the artistic objects around her with fresh eyes. Like the Coronation coach, she discovered, nearly every piece of Palace furniture had its history and, despite the massing of family ancestors in every room, there were still missing and long-sought portraits of bygone kith-and-kin to enrich every sales catalogue with romantic prospects, like the treasure chart of a desert island.

In Queen Mary's sparkling sitting-room at Marlborough House were objects that would have enchanted any child — a tiny Fabergé grand piano carved in jade, a rose quartz Buddha with a nodding head of jewelled chalcedony, a crystal swan, miniature animals in platinum and diamonds. Such treasures alerted the young Princess to the possible beauty of the smallest bibelot. On visits to Windsor Castle she had, of course, been permitted a personal inspection of the Queen's Dolls' House, that extraordinary miniature built at a scale of an inch to a foot and designed, as Sir Edwin Lutyens said, to "enable future generations to see how a King and Queen of England lived in the twentieth century and what authors, artists and craftsmen of note there were during the reign". The Princess could handle minute paintings by William Nicholson, Orpen, and Munnings, and turn the delicate pages of albums an inch square with seven hundred watercolours and drawings by other artists of eminence.

The Princess was one of the few people allowed to open the stamp-sized books and perhaps read the contribution by Kipling (a miniature "If") and some others. Bernard Shaw was indeed the only notable absentee of over 200 writers of the day thus represented, and the Princess was taught to regard the dolls' house as the ingenious treasure coffer it is, in no sense a plaything.

From Queen Mary's lips, too, our present Queen first heard still more of the stories of the objects and pictures in the royal collections which she now noticeably enjoys telling in turn to others. There is at Windsor, for example, both a Zoffany portrait of George III and a copy of the same painting worked in needlework by Mary Knowles, the eighteenth-century Quaker. Through the good offices of a dealer, Queen Mary discovered and acquired a self-portrait in needlework by Mary Knowles showing her at work on the George III embroidery itself. Such triumphant acquisitions frequently seasoned the everyday news between the grandmother and attentive granddaughter.

With King George VI upon the Throne, his new Queen also now raised a banner of artistic appreciation and encouragement as one of her first definitive acts in the shadow role of Queen Consort. It was announced that Her Majesty had bought two twentieth-century British paintings for the royal collections and that other pictures would be similarly purchased from time to time. The first painting thus honoured was indeed contemporary only in the narrow sense that the artist was one of only four living painters represented at a current exhibition of British painting in the Louvre. It was, in fact, one of Wilson Steer's Chepstow Castle compositions, painted in 1906, which has its kindred in the Tate Gallery and elsewhere. The royal patron, however, freshly admired the brilliant effect of sunlight and perhaps hoped that the purchase would cheer and comfort the painter faced, as he was, with encroaching blindness and despondency. After visiting Windsor, while on Royal Academy business, Sir William Llewellyn was, in fact, able to give the ailing Steer pleasure by reporting the "anxious care" that had been bestowed upon the hanging of his work.

The Queen's second purchase, *The Sleeping Philosopher* by Augustus John, the study of the dozing Bernard Shaw, was greeted with irony by *The Times*. "A sense of humour, if nothing else, should restrain a subject from commending the Queen upon her taste and judgment," rasped its art critic. The Queen liked to bring her daughter into family conversations, and we can hardly imagine that this faint praise passed without discussion.

However, not to over-colour this account of a trained discrimination, there is no record of Princess Elizabeth privately visiting any London art galleries with her mother, although the Queen soon also acquired a Matthew Smith still life, *Jugs and Fruit*, and bought another of Augustus John's portrait studies, *Ida Nettleship and Dorelia*, from Messrs. Tooth's gallery. William Nicholson's *The Golden Jug*, a sea piece by Ethel Walker, Sickert's famous *Ennui* and his *Fancy Dress Ball* also enriched the walls of Royal Lodge at this time, and the Queen derived especial delight and pride from possessing an impressionist Alfred Sisley *The Seine near St. Cloud*. An effective if small selection of the paintings of the first third of the twentieth century thus surrounded Queen Elizabeth II in her girlhood. In the sitting-room at 145 there usually stood an easel with a current offering from one of the galleries and, under her mother's thoughtful and appreciative guidance, the immense spread and weight of the Crown collections was never allowed to become burdensome or oppressive.

III

The future Queen was, of course, accustomed more than any other child to all the mediums of portraiture. The disciplines imposed on the sitter, the unique relationship often quickly established with painter or sculptor, the persuasive influence upon the viewer, all built up an explicit and habitual association with the arts from the very roots of youthful memory. The Princess had been painted for a miniature by Mabel Hankey at the age of three; she had been painted by Edmund Brock when only four and the portrait hung over the mantelpiece in the morning-room at 145 Piccadilly. At seven she sat composedly for Philip de Laszlo: "intelligent and full of character" he remembered her, "but very sleepy and restless at the second sitting, having attended Queen Mary's birthday luncheon party".

The Princess Elizabeth was indeed only nine when she visited an artist's studio (apparently for the first time) to play her part in the pageantry of her first occasion picture, Frank Salisbury's *Jubilee Thanksgiving Service of George V in St. Paul's*. It was one of those crowded canvases in which the likeness of as many people as possible must be depicted with rigid fidelity; the two little Princesses are prominent in the foreground, and for the detailed work Princess Elizabeth and her sister went out to Sarum Chase, the artist's huge new-built mock Tudor home on what was then one of the last unbuilt pinnacles of Hampstead Heath. To a child it was probably very like exchanging one castle for another. The studio itself was artfully designed to convey the heraldic sense of history, even to the royal arms in plaster in the central scroll of the ceiling, and as the artist worked he dramatically told his sitters that a beacon had been lit on this very hill to carry the news of the Spanish Armada.

Before her father's Coronation, the Princess was also modelled by Siegmund Strobl, the Hungarian sculptor, who found her climbing on to his pedestal fully determined to pose for an hour if necessary. A trifle nonplussed at her assurance, the sculptor suggested that she could sit or move, as she wished. "Thank you very much," the Princess responded, with a touch of finality. "Then I shall move about." The typical atmosphere of the studio was quickly and effortlessly assimilated. Visiting Margaret Lindsay Williams early the following year, the young sitter had an observant eye for technicalities. "And what is that for?" she asked, eyeing the turps. "And what is this, please?" taking up a palette knife.

Princess Elizabeth was thirteen when she first visited the Royal Academy. This was in May, 1939, only three days after the King and Queen had sailed for Canada, and she came noticeably unaccompanied by her younger sister. It was as if the Heiress Presumptive significantly found herself the first lady in the land and took great pains to select an official duty which should be specially fitting for the first engagement, her first also made in her own right and the first undertaken in her teens. If there had been adult prompting, it also pleasantly happened that the Summer Exhibition of 1939 was auspiciously encouraging to the tyro. It was an unassuming and friendly show, that year, with familiar portraits to make her feel in homely territory. The State Portraits of her father and mother by James Gunn dominated the scene, while the colder sculptures were grouped about the proposed memorial figures of her grandfather. There were landscapes by Gerald Kelly; a characteristic, strong and humorous *Gypsy Grandmother* by Laura Knight and an exceptional portrait of Hilaire Belloc by James Gunn. Subconsciously this may have influenced Princess Elizabeth ten years later when she took such pride in owning the sketch of the conversation piece by Gunn depicting Belloc, G. K. Chesterton, and Maurice Baring. On one of the walls there also hung Lawrence's *Queen Elizabeth Visits Her Army at Tilbury*, and perhaps she vividly remembered its pageantry after twenty years on seeing it again in Colchester Town Hall when she was Queen Elizabeth herself.

The youthful royal visitor was ushered round the Academy with tact, sympathy, and insight, far removed in spirit from the churlishness with which Benjamin Haydon showed Queen Victoria, as a Princess aged barely 13, around an exhibition of his paintings at the Egyptian Hall. "She has not much taste for high art or for high poetry," he wrote savagely to Wordsworth. "She and her mother came to see my *Xenophon*, which they did not understand, but they laughed heartily at my *Reading The Times*." In Princess Elizabeth's case, the experiment clearly was rewarding. Further excursions were made to the London art exhibitions in that last childhood summer of peace until, in July, these culminated in a visit to the exhibition of Royal and Historic Treasures which was being staged under charitable auspices at 145 Piccadilly, the Princess's old home. This experience must have been extremely strange: to find the familiar old rooms stripped of much that was remembered and refurnished with trophies of the artistic chase, to see the old doorways newly labelled "Their Majesties' Dining Room", "The Queen's Boudoir", "The Royal Nursery", "Princess Margaret's Room", as if the Queen's Dolls' House were expanding suddenly to life size, to move through crowds of whispering people and find one's old dolls scattered over the nursery floor. This last was for display purposes, and would never have been permitted in the old days, and on the wall was a childhood drawing by George V that had not been there before. Downstairs the Princess could find her mother's writing desk back in its usual place, but fine pieces of furniture from other sources were marshalled like alien strangers in her father's panelled study.

A photograph taken of the occasion seems to implement the impression that the Princess was confused and even intimidated by this dreamlike and somewhat macabre adventure. The treasures on show had been gathered from homes all over Britain as well as from royal sources: Turner's paint-daubed palette was displayed in curious partnership with the screens worked by Mary Queen of Scots while a prisoner at Sheffield; chinoiserie tapestries formed an elaborate background for such mementos as the Duke of Wellington's shaving mug, for one of Lord Baldwin's pipes and the knitting that had dropped from Emily Brontë's hand as she died. Captain Oates's sleeping-bag ranked with a jewel worn by Napoleon, paintings were equated with Queen Elizabeth's petticoat and the trivia of royal dressing-tables. Nevertheless this confused but popular exhibition may well have imposed on the impressionable Princess a fresh sense of the historic value and sustained interest of even the smallest treasures in the royal collections. As it turned out, moreover, other circumstances were to imprint this curious and eccentric exhibition on her memory. She did not know that she was visiting 145 for the last time and taking leave of her childhood. She did not realize that another chapter in her life had already opened. Yet it was in this week that Princess Elizabeth also visited Dartmouth College with the King and so first met her future husband.

3: THE RETURN FROM THE CAVES

I

The outbreak of war found Princess Elizabeth at Birkhall, the small comfortable Georgian house to the east of Balmoral. At that date faded Spy cartoons of half-forgotten statesmen lined the staircase and mainly amateur drawings of Scottish scenery dotted the walls, and in this homely atmosphere schoolroom studies progressed as usual. The Princess was studying history — by mail — under Henry Marten, reading Milton with Marion Crawford, and singing French duets with Princess Margaret under their French teacher, Mrs. Montaudon-Smith. But the Princess Elizabeth was also reading omnivorously, if not every book in the house then at least the fresher books that constantly arrived by post or were bought at Ballater.

The preparation of *The Queen's Book of the Red Cross*, particularly, was a fund-raising project just at this time that, of course, commanded her immediate interest, and from Sandringham at Christmas she sent a number of gift copies to her friends. With an introductory letter in facsimile from the Queen, here were stories and essays by some thirty authors, among them C. Day-Lewis, Daphne du Maurier, D. L. Murray, Howard Spring, L. A. G. Strong, Jan Struther, H. M. Tomlinson, and Hugh Walpole. The poems were by John Masefield, Alfred Noyes, T. S. Eliot, and Walter de la Mare, and the contributing artists included Rex Whistler, Edmund Blampied, Russell Flint, Bip Pares, Norman Wilkinson, Arthur Wragg, Laura Knight, and Edmund Dulac.

The Princess was acquainted with many of these names already, in a personal context. She knew, what many people did not, for example, that Edmund Dulac had designed the cameo portraits of the King on the current postage stamps, and she had seen and admired a sumptuous copy of *Sir John Vanbrugh* with hand-decorated end papers by Rex Whistler, which had been a presentation to her mother. In the hope, so widely shared early in the war, of carrying on as usual for as long as possible, the Queen herself resolutely continued to visit the London art exhibitions. When the family returned to Royal Lodge in 1940 the Princess was able to see the two paintings bought from Duncan Grant's one-man show at Agnew's, his small picture of Newhaven Pier and his beautiful study of St. Paul's from across the river, which the critics had acclaimed. Some of the modern pictures from Royal Lodge were also loaned to an exhibition of British painting at the National Gallery, yet all too short a time remained for the sensitive claims of art in the darkening world. With the Nazi invasion of the Netherlands in May, the young Princesses had to transfer to the congealed and austere atmosphere of Windsor Castle, and here they felt the icy finger of artistic loss.

All the major works of art had disappeared into safe hiding; the unrivalled Canalettos and Zoffanys from the broad corridor, the Hoppners from the White Drawing Room, even the sporting Stubbs and Ben Marshalls from King George VI's sitting-room. The masterpieces by Rubens and Van Dyck, Holbein and Rembrandt had, of course, been removed from the State Apartments, which now bore an empty, desolate, and haunted air. Substituted prints and watercolours came into greater prominence in the private rooms, but still there were gaps where Chippendale mirrors, precious clocks and display cabinets had left the shadowed traces of their presence. Many royal treasures were stored in strong boxes in the Sally Port; others found safe hospitality in remote country houses. It was typical of the fate of the scattered collections that the valuable porcelain from Buckingham Palace spent the war in a disused tunnel of the Aldwych underground railway, and, as the war deepened in savage intensity, still greater safety for the more precious paintings was found with the National Gallery collections in the air-conditioned chambers that had been built within the cavernous workings of the Manod slate quarries in Wales. At a susceptible age the future Queen thus vividly shared the artistic deprivation which the whole nation experienced, though to a keener personal degree. Gone were the refined Gainsborough ladies, the rigid Lawrence generals, the lively Dutch interiors, the deep Claude landscapes, even the sweet rapt sentiment of the Winterhalters. She had counted these gazing figures almost as her friends, the landscapes an extension of the living countryside, and now they seemed all the more to belong to a glittering prismatic past, as vanished and bygone as the street lights.

Even this stringent phase was, however, to prove productive. As if war stung the civic conscience, a Ministry of Labour committee put forward a scheme for engaging artists in capturing the characteristic landscape and architecture of the British scene before town and country suffered change by bombing or invasion. The royal collections have always been peculiarly wanting in the school of topographical English watercolours, other than the work of Alexander Cozens and that foundation pair, Paul and Thomas Sandby, and the Recording Britain scheme caught Princess Elizabeth's imagination. It was irksome that the bombing of London in 1941 saw her denied permission to visit the first selection of resulting drawings at the National Gallery. The present Queen Mother attended the exhibition, however, admired among others the Berkshire sketches of John Piper, and hit on a pleasant compensation to her daughter by commissioning him to prepare a set of twelve watercolour records of Windsor Castle. Working in the autumn, the artist found the grim, gaunt courtyards in sympathy with the mood of stormy backgrounds and harsh Gothic enhancement that prevailed at that time in his sketchbooks. ("What wretched weather you had!" the King sympathized, or so the story goes, viewing his Windsor drawings afterwards.) In her sixteenth year the Princess was intrigued by the thin, ascetic figure of the painter, whom she glimpsed from time to time at work in the quadrangles and gateways. When twelve further drawings were ordered it was said that the commission included one picture especially for her, but the Queen has no significant remembrance of the matter. What is more certain is that her knowledge of her mother's tastes was acquiring a firmer and more fruitful depth of understanding.

Two years later her mother purchased the Paul Nash picture, *The Landscape of the Vernal Equinox*, which was later to gain celebrity as one of the four works representing British painting in the Lion and Unicorn Pavilion at the South Bank Exhibition, the other three being by Hogarth, Gainsborough, and Constable. "I have had the peculiar honour of being bought by the Queen," Paul Nash wrote pleasurably to a friend. But his satisfaction would have been enhanced had he known that Princess Elizabeth shortly afterwards bought his painting, *The Forest*. With its distinct vertical design of grey and dark trees, an evocation of the steep hillsides of oak and beech around St. Paul's Walden, the Princess perhaps intended the picture as a gift to her mother. Shortly afterwards she herself was given Paul Nash's *Charcoal Burners* and she was also soon to have a third Paul Nash, one of the *Cloud Flora* watercolours, at Clarence House.

When the Princesses' wartime amateur pantomimes were held in the Waterloo Chamber at Windsor Castle, the empty frames of the Lawrence portraits proved too great a temptation and were soon filled with pantomime posters, Mother Goose replacing the Duke of Wellington and Dick Whittington stepping into the frame of Field-Marshal Blucher. "How do you like my ancestors?" King George VI inquired, gravely pointing to these ludicrous figures when he showed someone round. As the war drew to a close, however, the post-war rehabilitation of his collection actively interested the King; and when the Royal Academy made a proposal that a selection of his pictures might be shown to the public before being re-hung in Buckingham Palace and Windsor Castle he readily assented. The winter exhibition of the King's pictures filled the eleven galleries and central hall of Burlington House in the bitter winter of 1946–7 and overflowed into three other rooms, a superbly successful exhibition visited by 366,832 people. The hanging committee, with a nucleus of Sir Gerald Kelly, Anthony Blunt, Ellis Waterhouse, and Benedict Nicolson, had performed the invidious task of selecting five hundred works, from Tudor portraiture through the many masterpieces of the greatest painters in Europe — Venetian, Italian, Flemish, Dutch, French — to the Victorian subject pictures and the final Landseer pastels. But first one must mention that when wartime restrictions on the movements of Princess Elizabeth ended on May 15th, 1945, seven days after the end of hostilities in Europe, the Princess at once accompanied her parents on their visit to the exhibition of the first fifty paintings, including masterpieces by Botticelli, Michelangelo, and Rembrandt, restored to the National Gallery. Even before this — indeed, two days after the death of Hitler — she had visited the preview of the Royal Academy summer exhibition with the King and Queen, ostensibly to see the long-delayed Gerald Kelly State portraits of the King and Queen in Coronation robes, but also to devote noticeable attention to the work of Rodrigo Moynihan, Anthony Devas, Philip Connard, Ruskin Spear, and Edward Wadsworth.

Such was the mark of immediate recognition and respect royally paid to art in the dawning of the peace. The sustained and enlarging plans for the exhibition of the King's pictures then formed a constant topic through the following year. Pictures which had been cleaned and restored with notable results, such as Holbein's portrait of the young Cologne merchant, *Derich Born*, came to the Palace week by week to be separately displayed, a stimulating procession that quickened the King's appreciation and interest and constantly delighted his family. Gainsborough's opalescent group of the three eldest daughters of George III was freshly hung in the King's Audience Room, where it presumably proved a more soothing influence to visiting ambassadors than the antagonisms of the Delaroche Napoleons or Meissonier's *La Rixe*.

At Windsor, similarly, new arrangements were made for the fifteen small oval portraits of the family of George III to be hung massed together with frames touching to the precise arrangement Gainsborough had originally proposed for them, while the Queen equally decided that a set of four Fête Champetre studies by Jean Baptiste Pater should henceforth be close to her in her sitting-room. All this active concern for the royal paintings reached a climax for the Royal Family in October, 1946, when the King and Queen and the two Princesses returned from Balmoral and attended an evening party at Burlington House as the private preview of the King's exhibition.

The King declared jokingly that he did not know he owned so many fine pictures. The works had, in fact, never before been hung in order from period to period, first the newly luminous portraits of Tudor times, the Holbeins and his followers, next the portraits from Charles I onwards, passing from the Van Dycks to the Gainsboroughs, the Lelys to the portraits by Zoffany and Reynolds and Lawrence. Princess Elizabeth had never before seen the great collection of Italian pictures — the Giorgiones, the Titians, the Tintorettos, the works of Andrea del Sarto and so many others — assembled together from Windsor Castle, Hampton Court, and Buckingham Palace. She may well have paused before the anonymous contemporary portrait of Queen Elizabeth I as Princess, the only certain contemporary portrait of the Queen as Princess that has come down to us. At the gate of womanhood she recognized with delight the Flemish and Dutch pictures which she had known so well before the interminable years of war, and the Canalettos, nearly forty studies of Venice and London and Rome, the pick of Antonio Canale's production, brought together in a single room.

Nor were these pictures the drugging assembly of a single evening's pleasure. Through the winter the King gave a series of memorable private parties at Burlington House, the enjoyment of his guests sharpened by being among the first social occasions since the war. Refreshments were served in the splendid Assembly Room, with its painted ceiling, its great Constable landscape, its Sheraton sideboards glinting with silver and the glowing colours of hothouse tulips. At these parties the Princess met many senior painters and sculptors of the day — Augustus John, Sir William Reid Dick, Sir Alfred

Munnings, Sir W. Russell Flint, Dame Laura Knight, Harold Knight, Charles Wheeler, Charles Cundall — and so many others. The conversation was not repressed. Sir Anthony Blunt, Surveyor of the King's — later the Queen's — Pictures, was remembered pointing his finger at a full-length by Reynolds and declaring roundly that Picasso was immeasurably a finer artist. It completed the Princess's youthful education to hear the views of others on her father's pictures, to discover that reputations were not sacrosanct and to learn that the resurgent art world shook in a ferment of change. The last of these evening parties was held only two days before the Royal Family sailed on their 1947 tour of South Africa. It was a happy augury, surely, that the artists of five centuries and of our own day should have thus embroidered the background of our present Queen's life at the crucial time when she had fallen deeply in love.

III

When the Royal Family returned from South Africa, and Princess Elizabeth returned home to her betrothal, most of the royal paintings had already been restored to their appointed places on palace and castle walls, and State Rooms and private apartments alike glowed anew with their life and colour. These benign and domestic Presences after so long an absence illumined and heightened the Princess's personal happiness. The finer pieces of furniture had returned, too, like long-lost friends, and it is significant that as the months to the Princess's wedding day sped by, the friends and relatives who knew her best sought to meet her pleasure in beautiful things. Among the jewels, the gleaming pieces of antique furniture, the Steuben crystal and fine china of the wedding gifts, there were also over sixty oil paintings and drawings ranging from a

Constable sepia sketch of Brighton beach to one of the *Cloud Flora* watercolours of Paul Nash.

There were presents that indulged the Princess's historical tastes, such as Winterhalter's pencil sketch for the large family picture at Osborne, George Dawes's watercolour sketch of Princess Charlotte of Wales (probably the original of the portrait in the National Gallery) and Count D'Orsay's tinted drawing of Queen Victoria, perhaps the very one mentioned in Frith's reminiscences. Lord Fairhaven precisely gauged the mechanism of pleasure when he gave a Paul Sandby gouache *Windsor on a Rejoicing Night*, the first of the many Sandbys since collected by the Queen. Then there were pictures of personal memento, such as the oil paintings of H.M.S. *Vanguard*, by Norman Wilkinson and Frank Beresford, Nigel Mould's painting of the royal corgis, *Crackers and Sue*, a Munnings study of the Princess mounted at the Trooping the Colour ceremony, and many more. But there were also pictures by Wilson Steer, Paul Maze, Edward Seago, Lamorna Birch, Hans Tisdall, Feliks Topolski and others sufficient to form the nucleus of a new collection. Like other brides, Princess Elizabeth faced the problem of arranging these gifts to the best advantage when she furnished her home at Clarence House: where to put Barney Seale's bronze bust of Augustus John, where best to hang the Hollar engravings of London. (Fortunately some difficulty was foreseen by the donor of a fragment of the Holy Carpet from the great Mosque at Mecca, and it was presented framed under glass to form a tray.)

When Clarence House came to be occupied in 1949, the furnishings represented less the Princess's individual taste than her taste as it was seen by others. Yet the harmonious arrangement of the pieces was hers, and the fine finish of the decor was in response to her own meticulous demands, the matching perfection of her own ideas. In the Nash entrance hall a spacious modern river scene took pride of place with a Sheraton table clock, a seventeenth-century Verona wedding chest, a Chippendale table and airily elegant crystal chandeliers. In the adjacent dining-room a series of small portraits of William IV's brothers and sisters and parents had been removed to safety during the war, yet they had been incorporated within the plasterwork mouldings of the decorative scheme for as long as living memory could tell and the Princess satisfied her sense of history by directing that they should be returned. The frames and reliefs were now picked out in white, on her instructions, and to obtain the exact shade of the apple-green of the walls she herself helped to mix the paint. It was a matter of pride to her to own a dining-table signed by Casement in 1770: but the accompanying ladder-back chairs seemed too numerous and she carried one or two out to the hall.

The drawing-room, though endowed with Nash ceilings and chimneypieces, had originally been two intercommunicating rooms, and the two halves, still partly divided by two columns, were of unequal size. This difficulty troubled the Princess until the Duke of Edinburgh suggested that the walls of one portion should be of ivory with mouldings of pale grey while the smaller portion reversed the scheme with pale grey walls and ivory mouldings. The variation successfully produced a subtle unity and, since this was a room for formal social occasions, the Princess chose Aubusson carpets in old rose and aquamarine blue, and a set of painted and gilt settees and chairs in the Louis XV taste, upholstered in aquamarine silk, with satinwood predominating in the side-tables and other furniture.

But it was in the Princess's sitting-room — her everyday living-room — that one found all the tell-tale touches that afford clues to her character: the radiogram between armchair and fireplace, the magazine rack handy beside the settee, the photo-cluttered yet decidedly utilitarian Chippendale writing desk by the big window. A satinwood chest of drawers of bedroom style, though admittedly circa 1780, stood ready to receive odds and ends. In colour the walls were a delicate pale blue with a hint of green, the Chinese carpet predominantly of pale golden tone, the two armchairs and sofa of flowered chintz in shades of blue. The furniture was not in careful matching unison, but consisted chiefly of the young couple's closest, most personal wedding gifts. One may mention a dark mahogany Hepplewhite breakfast bookcase which had been jointly the gift of members of the Royal Family, a smaller bookcase large enough only for books of current reading and reference, and a superlative four-fold screen embroidered with Chinese scenes in blue and gold which had been the gift of Queen Mary. The Princess had also replaced the ornate marble and ormolu chimneypiece with the more contemporary taste of carved pine.

The room, though not excessively large — only thirty-two feet by nineteen — was sufficiently spacious to absorb the larger pieces of furniture, while small enough for a sense of cosiness and comfort. At night, when the damask curtains were closed, light sparkled richly from the cut-glass chandelier and the silk-shaded wall sconces, or could be dimmed to only one or two table lamps. As Queen, Her Majesty has complained humorously that she is apt to be allergic to her own likeness, but as Princess she hung Edward Halliday's portrait of herself where it could best be seen. This is the original study for the full-length now in the London Drapers' Hall and the Princess later matched it in her room with Halliday's companion portrait of her husband, when the piece was finished. The other pictures in her sitting-room, at the very nucleus of her young married life, also merit regard. To the left of the fireplace there hung James Gunn's sketch in oils for his conversation piece of Hilaire Belloc, G. K. Chesterton, and Maurice Baring. The finished larger canvas of the three figures has been seen by thousands while on loan to the National Portrait Gallery; and a connecting link of filial sentiment may be recognized in the portrait of Hilaire Belloc by Augustus John which the Queen Mother owned.

On the other side of the fireplace there also hung a small oil painting by Charles Cundall, an impression of the Forum in Rome, an attractive picture of half-shadowed columns beneath a pellucid sky. A shore scene by Robin Goodwin was also, one suspects, a highly acceptable gift claiming its right to a special place in her room. So also, no doubt, was the little scene from *Le Lac des Cygnes* which hung opposite the Princess's desk, where she had but to lift her eyes to drink in its charming grace and romance. Placed as if it were one of her favourite pictures, it satisfied her sense of discipline, represented her love of the ballet and her affection for the donor and, though she could not know this, it accommodated a latent element of the future, for the artist was none other than Oliver Messel, uncle of a certain Antony Armstrong-Jones, later Lord Snowdon.

As Christopher Hussey has said, the selection of pictures sustained the principal part in creating the contemporary atmosphere of Clarence House. Aside from wedding gifts, the work of Sidney Causer, Duncan Grant, Rowland Hilder, William Haggett, William Lamb and others were awarded prominence. When the queen, as Princess Elizabeth, became chatelaine of the old mansion she was still only twenty-three years old. Her tastes and those of her husband were still in an early formative phase. (They made a joint light-hearted experiment in collecting by forming a small gallery of modern caricatures and cartoons, with the original work of H. M. Bateman, Fougasse, Osbert Lancaster, Giles and others.) While the improvement of Clarence House was still in progress, however, the Princess consented to undertake a public duty which was to bring her into close and sympathetic contact with the most emergent and enterprising painters, sculptors and designers of the day.

IV

When the Queen's great-great-grandfather, the Prince Consort, became President of the Society of Arts in 1847 and procured it a Royal Charter, he did not foresee the sequel of events that were so rapidly to lead him to sponsor the Great Exhibition in Hyde Park. On the other hand, when the Princess Elizabeth became President of the Royal Society of Arts precisely a century later, she anticipated with eager interest the prospects of an exhibition to commemorate the centenary of the endeavours of 1851. Prince Albert merely "honoured with his presence" the meeting at the Royal Society of Arts at which the exhibition so closely connected with his name was first announced. He was indeed puzzled to read an announcement of "His Royal Highness's plans" and urgently summoned an official to Buckingham Palace to explain what was meant. But when the Council of the Festival of Britain 1951 met for the first time in the handsome Adam building still occupied by the Royal Society of Arts, Princess Elizabeth welcomed them as R.S.A. President and delivered the inaugural Festival address. Her speech was somewhat in the style of Sir Alan Lascelles, the King's Private Secretary, and yet bore the unmistakable stamp of revision by a younger hand. The Princess first reminded the Council that the 1851 exhibition had laid special emphasis on promoting the arts and sciences and on the application of the arts to industrial design. "It should be our object to do the same," she continued. "I would suggest to you the importance of setting the highest standards in everything you plan. This lays a special duty on our craftsmen and manufacturers... I hope that in emphasizing our achievements of the past and present you will stress no less sharply our responsibilities to the future. Then the Festival may prove to be not merely an end in itself, but the beginning of many good things..."

The Great Exhibition immortalized, in Queen Victoria's words, "Albert's dearest memory". Unburdening himself to his brother Ernst, the Prince Consort wrote of "our" exhibition and henceforth assumed the firm authorship. But for the protocol under which the King and Queen gave the Festival of Britain their patronage, Princess Elizabeth might similarly have spoken of "my" Festival and would indeed have received far more credit for her share. The reality of her sponsorship, and the energetic interest she gave to it, young as she was, is in fact little realized. Within limits she was active throughout as an organizer rather than an onlooker, energetically encouraging progress and suggesting ideas. Just as the Royal Society of Arts was chiefly responsible for the 1951 exhibition, so the 1951 Festival was born of the proposals of the Ramsden Committee, of Sir Gerald Barry and of the Royal Society of Arts and, as the R.S.A. secretary has summarized, "Princess Elizabeth brought all her particular gifts of youth, sincerity, gaiety and lively intelligence to the service of this ancient Society. It would be difficult to overestimate the importance of her contribution..."

The Princess inaugurated the Festival sitting in the very chair used by her great-great-grandfather. Thenceforth her keen interest marked the beginning of intimate acquaintance with Sir Hugh Casson, Sir Leigh Ashton, and Sir Gerald Barry — who came under a fire of searching questions when he lunched at Clarence House — Robin Darwin, of the Royal College of Arts, Lawrence Whistler and many others. If the Princess was considered by some to be thoroughly trammelled in academic tradition, she now became thoroughly versed in the rich new creative effects of Barbara Hepworth and Lynn Chadwick, Henry Moore and Graham Sutherland, Frank Dobson, Keith Godwin, Siegfried Charoux, Karel Vogel, and Victor Pasmore.

Feliks Topolski's mural *Cavalcade of Commonwealth* awakened a royal interest, as we know, that has been sustained to the present time; Kenneth Rowntree's mural in the Lion and the Unicorn Pavilion was to have an aftermath of recognition in his two pictures for the Queen's contemporary collection ten years later. Nor was the Princess's stimulus to the Festival limited to the lip-service of admiring interest. The King and Queen had to adopt the leading role in London at the dedication service, the inaugural concert, the tour of pavilions and courtyards through drizzling British rain, but the Princess's official duties varied from the opening of the great industrial exhibition at Glasgow to her attendance at the music and arts festival at Norwich and her visit to a similar Scottish festival in Perth. There were a score of other tasks almost too transient to mention, calling now for her alert and appreciative presence at a Festival concert of church music, now opening the R.S.A. "Exhibition of Exhibitions", now inspecting a "painting for pleasure" display. None of those who watched her realized that she would be Sovereign Queen within a year.

V

From 1948 onwards Princess Elizabeth had made a point of visiting the annual Antique Dealers Fair, and in Festival year she opened the Fair, explaining that she herself was only a

57

novice in the art of collecting and owed all the knowledge she possessed to the advice of her grandmother, Queen Mary.

This influence was then at the zenith of its strength. As James Pope-Hennessy has noted, Queen Mary would never have dreamed of initiating a collection of contemporary pictures. "Really extraordinary and very ugly," she chillingly dismissed the South Bank Exhibition. Sadly aware of fleeting time as she passed into her middle eighties, the old Queen nonetheless tried to encourage her children to follow her example and collect "family things", and sought to instil at least some knowledge she had acquired by painstaking reading and careful observation, and her eldest granddaughter did not escape the missionary zeal. Very characteristically, Queen Mary's christening gift to Prince Charles was a silver-gilt cup and cover which George III had given to a godson in 1780, "so that I gave a present from my great-grandfather to my great-grandson 168 years later", as she recorded.

In conversation with Princess Elizabeth she inevitably also spoke of her own girlhood years in Florence, where her early studies in art had been founded, and so kindled in her granddaughter a desire to visit that beautiful city, if not to undertake a modified grand tour. Both ambitions were realized in the year before Princess Elizabeth came to the throne. A Christmas stay with her husband in Malta provided an opportunity to visit Greece early in the New Year and a month at Easter afforded time for seeing both Florence and Rome.

In Athens the eager cameramen may have marred the Princess's enjoyment of the Parthenon, but a week of less hustled sightseeing was devoted to such sites as the Palace of Agamemnon at Mycenae, the ancient theatre at Epidavros, the temples of Poseidon and Apollo. In Rome, staying at the British Embassy, the Princess showed herself a meticulous and studious tourist, as if all her previous education had primed her receptivity to the classical round. Visiting the Forum, she found the picture by Charles Cundall which had so long hung before her in her sitting-room tangibly realized in reality. No official programme was pressed upon her and the Princess elected to devote a day in the Borghese Gallery. Here was Bernini's *David*, Van Dyck's *Descent from the Cross*, and Titians and Raphaels in abundance to gain her already informed attention.

Next, her stay in Florence saw repeated visits to the Pitti and Uffizi galleries. "We visited five saloons very carefully. Titians! Raphaels! Andrea del Sartos! Van Dycks! Rubenses — gloriously beautiful! Quite beyond everything!" So the old Duchess of Teck had gushed during Queen Mary's youthful visits. But Princess Elizabeth had cause for closer, more searching comparisons. Though so rich, the royal collections have nothing by Botticelli, no paintings by Leonardo da Vinci or Ghirlandaio, and here was a feast. In the small Royal Closet at Buckingham Palace where the Royal Family assemble for State occasions there hangs a fragment of a picture of the school of Filippo Lippi once so overpainted that when it was cleaned a background of rocks was proved to cover an entire landscape and showed the style closer to Fra Filippo than had been thought. We may suppose this tiny advance had its place in the Princess's thoughts as she filled her mind with the flowering of Florentine genius, the ransom of an early summer afternoon.

The Princess celebrated her twenty-fifth birthday in Rome, driving out with Prince Philip to explore the gardens of the Villa d'Este and Hadrian's Villa. When the young couple returned home, the journey had proportionately trained their powers of judgment. As Prince Philip sat for his portrait to

Edward Halliday, he raised the possibility of ringing the changes in royal portraiture. Why not a series of informally posed "conversation pieces" that would capture the pleasant atmosphere of everyday life at Clarence House with their young family? The painter and the royal couple became enthusiastic at the prospect of thus striking a new note. Nearly twelve years had passed since James Gunn recorded a similar conversation piece at Royal Lodge. But there seemed to be all the time in the world for experiment and when the Princess and her husband departed on that fateful flight to Kenya, Edward Halliday had the freedom of Clarence House for his preliminary studies of decor and furnishing. He imagined, as they did, that a vista of months lay ahead, but within eight days King George VI was dead and Elizabeth was Queen.

The golden dream of those pleasant pictures of Clarence House had gone for ever. The plans were indeed altogether shelved for several weeks, but both the Queen and the Duke of Edinburgh decided that one picture at least should be completed. At half-past nine on Thursday, April 10th, Halliday presented himself at Clarence House and found the Queen and Prince Philip in their sitting-room. The children were brought in and, while Princess Anne played with her toys on the floor, Prince Charles snuggled on the settee with a picture book beside his mother. The reading lamp was tipped to what the Queen called "our angle", the two corgi dogs completed the family circle. On the corner of his canvas Halliday inscribed the words "Maundy Thursday, 1952". From this domestic setting the Queen left for the Maundy service at Westminster Abbey, the first public engagement of her reign. That night she slept at Windsor and she did not return to Clarence House. The picture was exhibited by the Royal Society of Portrait Painters later that year and the Queen, in whose possession it remains, allowed it to be included in a touring exhibition of conversation pieces in 1962. But a royal portrait of equal intimacy has never been seen again.

4: THE QUEEN'S PICTURES

I

When the Queen first planned to show her paintings and other works of art to the public in the new Queen's Gallery at Buckingham Palace, imaginatively realizing an idea originally proposed by King George VI, the space was scheduled for selections of thirty to forty paintings at a time. If the selection were changed every month, each picture would need to appear only once in twenty years, so large is the royal collection, and since the display includes items from the enormous treasury of Old Master drawings from the Royal Library at Windsor — by Raphael, Leonardo, and Michelangelo, among others — the ever-varying show might outlast our century without repetition. In practice, the time may be even longer, for experience now shows that only two or three exhibitions are likely to be held each year.

The Queen's great-grandfather, King Edward VII, resented with indignation any suggestion that the royal collections were in any way national possessions, as if such hints of ownership were the thin end of a republican wedge. But the Queen has seemed from the first to regard herself more as the steward than the owner of her pictures, anxious for them to be seen and shared as much as possible and even distributed on loan as widely and generously as may be consistent with the exclusive dignity of the Crown.

The Queen indeed holds the bulk of her paintings and drawings "in right of the Crown" and not otherwise. The Rembrandts at Buckingham Palace and the Rubens and Van Dycks at Windsor are as much an impersonal and inalienable attachment to the Crown as the bulk of the Crown Jewels in the Tower of London. On the other hand, most of the paintings presented to Her Majesty in the course of her reign, including many from the Commonwealth, are considered her personal possessions, unless and until she chooses to make them over into the permanent Crown collections.

Without unduly emphasizing the difference, the Queen elects to keep many of her gift pictures at Sandringham and Balmoral. These are residences she similarly enjoys as her private family property, unlike Buckingham Palace or Windsor Castle, which she occupies by virtue of her position as head of the State. The distinction is the same as that between the Crown Jewels and the Queen's personal jewellery. The latter could be willed or given away or sold without affecting the separate durable character of the State Regalia. On occasion, aware of gaps in the Windsor art catalogues, the Queen has purchased pictures privately — for example, a set of six watercolours by Paul Sandby — which she acquired via the saleroom — and has then presented them to the Crown collection. Such gifts are as signed and documented nowadays as anything requiring precise legal definition, the transfer to the Crown being signified when a painting passes under the care of the Lord Chamberlain. Every Court official understands the salient boundaries of the Queen's dual ownership, but a member of the Household tells me that he has never seen it officially set forth or explained.

The last great shake-up of personal property versus the claims of royal sovereignty came after the death of Queen Victoria, when busts by the dozen were surveyed, only the finest passing into Crown care at Windsor, while the models in marble which the Queen had made of the hands and feet of her children passed into ghostly hiding in the private apartments at Osborne House.

In the old and overcrowded picture gallery at Buckingham Palace paintings that had hung skied and unobserved for decades at the level of the gas chandeliers were found to be sooted to opaque black, and some of the Queen's Oriental relics at Windsor were so insect-infested that they had to be burned. A store at Hampton Court yielded blackened and blistered portraits by Joshua Reynolds which had been damaged in a fire at Carlton House many years earlier. Carefully repaired and restored, they joined the noble collection of full-length portraits of the English school which now dignify the gallery leading to the State Supper Room.

With equal effect the remnants of the sumptuous suites of silver furniture presented to Charles II and William II — and shown at the Queen's Gallery — were retrieved from farmhouses and other buildings on the Windsor estate and placed in the Queen's Ballroom at the Castle, where they are usually to be found today as cherished as if they had never known such sad exile.

Under Edward VII, rearrangement was the order of the day. A line of ancestral portraits, from Henry VIII onward, was arrayed in the State Rooms at St. James's Palace, and an entire roll-call of military pictures mustered into a small collection (Crown) on the ground floor, where *The Defence of Rorke's Drift* and Caton Woodville's *Too Late* still intimidate visitors. Royal portraits and "occasions", from William and Mary to George III, were mainly relegated to Kensington Palace and the principle was laid down that pictures later than the eighteenth century should be removed from Hampton Court. Between his two identities of proprietorship, his crowned and private self, King Edward VII assessed his possessions with lenient fairness. His eldest sister remembered a small coloured bust of a child that had always stood on a cupboard in the nursery corridor, undeniably a private domain. The bust, when found, proved to be a study of a laughing boy — some think a dwarf — by Paganino, the Modena contemporary of Michelangelo who competed for the design of Henry VII's tomb in Westminster Abbey. The figure is now normally kept at Windsor under the Lord Chamberlain's auspices, but was loaned by the Queen to the 1962 Antique Dealers Fair.

Only copies of Winterhalter's famous family group and of his *Duchess of Kent* similarly remained at Osborne, while the originals were inscribed for the Crown collection and hung at Buckingham Palace. The king could justly have sold or privately retained the small collection of Spanish portraits which his mother had bought at auction to help the impoverished family of Louis Philippe, but he appears to have approved them for Crown care. Hung in the Belgian Suite, they long daunted foreign visitors until Queen Elizabeth II refurbished the rooms for the comfort of her guests. Rearranged to good effect, even the more depressing portraits of grandees were cheered by the effect of new rose and gold upholstery, and thus were preserved from the carefully tended store of temporarily banished pictures at Kensington Palace, where, with Stanfield and Watts and Leighton, crowded-out exiles usually find a home.

Fuller discussion revolved around the most personal pictures of all, the paintings that Queen Victoria had given to Prince Albert or vice versa on birthdays and other anniversaries, a parallel to the paintings that Prince Philip and Queen Elizabeth may have exchanged. Queen Victoria delighted her Albert on his twenty-fifth birthday, for instance, by giving him a much-restored portrait by Lucas Cranach. Though found "a complete wreck", this had passed under Crown auspices by the reign of George V. Many pictures that Albert had given Queen Victoria, however, remained in private hiding and somewhat in decay at Osborne, until in the present reign Queen Elizabeth II passed them into the care of the Ministry of Works.

Then there was the vexed question of the Oettingen-Wallerstein collection of primitives which the Prince Consort obligingly exhibited at Kensington Palace for the owner under the impression that the National Gallery might eagerly purchase them for the nation. When these hopes were not fulfilled, the disappointed Prince Consort bought the collection himself. After his death twenty-two of the pictures were given to the National Gallery, but at least ten are now in Crown care. In general, it can be assumed that works of art earlier than the first half of the nineteenth century have been assigned to the Crown collection, with later works of real or historic value, other than those of the last three reigns. The notable exceptions, of course, concern the private residences. Queen Alexandra's beloved portraits by Von Angeli remain at Sandringham; our own Queen has a friendly regard for the Landseers she privately owns at Balmoral.

When the pavilion at Aldershot was closed in 1962 the Queen was advised that the contents could be regarded as family property, but she decided to give the finer pieces to Brighton Pavilion, while others were offered to a local museum. Queen Mary enriched the Crown collection by buying and donating many fine pieces of furniture, though her predilection for Japanese incense burners and lacquered cabinets have disturbed later comers. On her death some of her lesser pieces of furniture and *objets d'art* were weeded out from Marlborough House and placed in the saleroom on the present Queen's instructions, but this was a hint of the limitations of both the capacity of the royal museum at Frogmore and of stringent royal finances under modern conditions. (Queen Adelaide's household goods were similarly auctioned at Marlborough House long, long ago.) The Sovereign is exempt from death duties and the Queen's family heirlooms have thus been spared the risks of dispersal forced on nearly all other great British collections. Members of the Royal Family are, however, more vulnerable. The collection of paintings of Queen Elizabeth the Queen Mother, her Manets and Sisleys and so forth, would be liable to valuation for probate, for example, unless she had presented them previously to the Crown.

Among the many notable instances of the Queen Mother's generosity we need cite only the magnificent suite of eighteenth-century gilt furniture in the Queen's Audience Chamber at Windsor Castle, which appears to have stood there since the days of George I and yet in reality was bought by the Queen Mother at the Stowe sale and presented by her to the Crown in 1939.

The submission of Queen Mary's "throw-outs" (as some called them) to the auction hammer contributed only £19,970 to her estate. But many of the pieces had been inherited from King Edward VII and Queen Alexandra and reflected the less virtuous taste of their own period of residence in Marlborough House. Victorian copies of florid Bourbon furniture were mixed with Regency rosewood console tables, and flamboyant Florentine cabinets of the late eighteenth century followed a pleasant Sheraton wardrobe. Some of the pieces were rather large — too large for souvenirs, critics complained — although a pair of cloisonne elephants nearly two feet high of the Ch'ien Lung period made 800 guineas. There was evidence of second thoughts in some of the items apparently withdrawn from sale, including the pair of mahogany bookcases which William Vile made for George II. Few of the true treasures of the commemorative exhibition of Queen Mary at the "V&A" Museum in 1954 were thrown on the market: one did not see her little Spencelayh pictures, her Matthew Boulton silver, her Tompion clocks. Neither was the portrait on glass of Queen Charlotte, which the Queen and the Duke of Edinburgh gave to Queen Mary, placed before the rude gaze of the world.

Inevitably, a special cachet attaches to royal property at auction. The Princess Royal and the Earl of Harewood realized £3,769 from forty-eight snuff-boxes offered at Christie's in 1957, some of which may have passed through Queen Mary's hands, the total being £31,356 in a two-day sale of snuff-boxes and objects of vertu. The Duke of Gloucester has sent snuff-boxes, porcelain and sporting books and pictures to the saleroom, but one must stress that when he acquired a first edition of *Alice in Wonderland* together with an autographed letter from Lewis Carroll, for £1,200, he passed them on to the British Museum at the price he had paid.

The Duke of Windsor cleared a little of his furniture, his Fabergé and his Japanese lacquer from Frogmore, and Princess Alice, Countess of Athlone, similarly demonstrated limitations of space at Kensington Palace in regard to old silver and decorative glass paperweights. The classic royal sale of more recent years was, however, the dispersal in 1947 of the late Duke of Kent's surplus pictures, porcelain, and furniture. As a younger son of Queen Mary, the Duke was always thought to possess considerable artistic knowledge and discrimination, and here the saleroom afforded the coldest assessment of his gifts, scarcely veiled by the upward trend of wartime inflation. The sale total of £92,300, however, represented twice his original outlay.

Though small by the standards of the 1960s, the sum of 6,600 guineas was paid for three noble Claude landscapes which the Duke had bought at auction for only 3,700 guineas seven years earlier. Yet we may note that the Duchess of Kent did not offer for sale the *Repose in Egypt* by Orazio Gentileschi which the Duke had purchased for under £400, nor the Van Bassen picture of Charles I dining in public which he had acquired in 1938 for only 170 guineas. Although these are lesser painters, the Duke may have reasonably argued that painters good enough for the patronage of Charles I were good enough for him.

It was Gentileschi who painted the elaborate ceilings of the Queen's House at Greenwich, which now roof the saloon of Marlborough House. They were sold for -£600 under Cromwell, a further oddity of fluctuating valuation, for the Crown appraisers priced all the seven Raphael cartoons at only £300 the set. The contrast with the £800,000 put upon the Royal Academy's Leonardo cartoon in 1962 tempts one into a profitless reverie on the modern value of the Crown collection. Even multiplying by twenty the £118,080 10*s.* 2*d.* at which the Commonwealth contemptuously valued the King's collection is clearly no approximation. An expert could more readily appraise the Cullinan Diamond or the Koh-i-Noor.

A study of the prices paid by George IV is equally fruitless, though closer to our time. The price he gave for the Palace's great Rembrandt *The Shipbuilder and His Wife* of £5,250 remained, for example, a saleroom record until 1893. His £3,990 for Van Dyck's *Christ Healing the Lame Man* stood unsurpassed until the opening year of the twentieth century itself. The £22,000 he paid to Sir Francis Baring in 1814 has an affluent modern ring, but this was for some seventy Dutch paintings, including incidentally a Rembrandt self-portrait and his *Adoration of the Magi*. Jacob van Ruisdael's *Evening Windmill* at £304 was high-priced in proportion. George IV is said to have bought Dutch and Flemish paintings chiefly because they were favoured by his friends, but he had a critical eye for the condition of paint and canvas, seldom buying anything that was not perfectly preserved, and his pictures are today among the finest works of the Buckingham Palace collection.

Four of the five Van Dycks at the Palace also represent the fruit of his enthusiasm and we need to remember that the great Rubens *The Farm at Laeken* was bought by the King after agents had refused it on his behalf. Nor did he omit the patronage of living artists. He once recorded that he had paid £24,000 in fees to Lawrence, and by comparison his artistic debts were trifling. Among other items we have the list "£1,050 to George Stubbs, £300 to George Romney; £352 to John Hoppner…" King George IV has been ceaselessly maligned for his lavish expenditure on works of art and remains an awful warning to the monarchy seven reigns later.

Nevertheless, as Sir Lionel Cust pointed out, when Buckingham Palace and Windsor Castle were newly furnished at the wish of Parliament for the better dignity of the Crown, the work was entrusted to a Royal Commission whose minions profitably proceeded to scrap, give away or banish nearly all the old English furniture. The costly and meretricious replacements installed by the Commission then steadily deteriorated until the greater part had to be scrapped during the renovations of Edward VII's reign.

Only the furniture, porcelain and pictures bought by George IV personally have continued to survive the pitfalls of changing taste and to increase in value, and indeed are still ranked among the finest of the Palace furnishings.

The monetary value of the Queen's works of art, however, remains an idle and worthless theme. A world record price of 34,000 guineas was once gained in the saleroom for a small Louis XV marquetry table by Oeben, the great French eighteenth-century craftsman. One is inclined to wonder what might be paid for the incomparably finer Louis XV bureau which stands in the White Drawing Room at the Palace and was the work of Riesener, who is generally considered Oeben's superior.

The Metropolitan Museum of New York similarly established what was then a world record in paying £821,400 for Rembrandt's *Aristotle* … and the Crown collection includes a dozen Rembrandts, including several of equal quality. We may recall the £275,000 paid for Rubens's *Adoration of the Magi*, and the Queen also owns at least five major Rubens works. Again, £143,000 has been paid for a Gainsborough, and the Queen as the Crown incarnate owns at least thirty, though not all of the same degree.

Far exceeding prices at the Duke of Kent's sale, the National Gallery has paid £47,000 for a Claude and the Queen possesses three of his greatest works. A Canaletto can readily reach £3,500. Thanks to George III's acquisition of the collection of Matthew Smith, who was English Consul in Venice, the Queen owns at least fifty-three Canaletto oil paintings and over a hundred drawings.

Equally the Crown collection embraces a score of Van Dycks, three works by Titian, seven paintings by Tintoretto (though mostly housed at Hampton Court with the Correggios and Bellinis) and, in another group, eight outstanding Jan Steens. Indeed, an expert assessed the value of the first forty pictures shown at the Queen's Gallery at over £5,000,000.

The catalogue of treasures could be continued almost indefinitely and their astronomical, constantly soaring value could be a matter of infinite debate and argument. We have seen enough to realize the richness and magnitude of the royal collections. We can begin to apprehend the sustaining effect upon the woman who lives as Queen in their midst. It is beyond dispute that no one of her disposition could share this environment without developing sound taste and judgment.

II

In the past, until the opening of the Queen's Gallery at Buckingham Palace, the Queen often demonstrated a regretful awareness that her pictures were being seen and enjoyed less than in the four previous reigns, even by the privileged few. The discontinuation of the Courts and Levees and the infrequency of State dinner parties had brought a new and undesired disuse to the State Apartments of the Palace. Even the scholar had inevitably become a less welcome figure under the insidious temptations of the miniature camera and the peril of newspaper memoirs which threatened royal privacy. Besides, the Palace has to be more efficient than of yore and there is courteous intention, but less ample time, for the admiration of pictures.

Convenience dictates, for example, that the 1844 Room is generally used for the Queen's luncheon parties. It normally contains the famous "Negress Head" clock from Carlton House and some of the fine Regency furniture that Queen Mary gave to the Crown collection, but on the walls the Winterhalters polish without notably enhancing the atmosphere. Again, only Winterhalters hang in the approaching Bow Room, although the Queen's superb Sèvres porcelain decorates the glazed recesses, and indeed it is possible for a luncheon guest to be ushered from the entrance and through the Marble Hall without being aware that the Queen cherishes more than an array of family portraits implemented by a battery of eighteenth-century side tables. Dinner guests are more fully entertained, and a usual venue is then the State Supper Room, linked as it is with the East Gallery, the Silk Tapestry Room and the Palace Picture Gallery itself. With fuller evening leisure at their disposal, the Queen and the Duke of Edinburgh genuinely delighted in showing their treasures to their guests, one of whom told me that he began the evening only with an impression of white and gold resplendence and ended by understanding the musical tastes of Gainsborough's son-in-law.

There are first, of course, the wonders of the Grand Staircase, if you have an eye for Regency bronze work or the spirited portraits of Dawe, Wilkie, and Hayter and, ascending to the East Gallery, one faces another blaze of portraits that perhaps few readily identify, though they are none the less impressive. Here is Copley's rich, vivacious masterpiece of George III's youngest daughters at play, outshining the heroic portrait groups by Benjamin West and dimming the Hoppners and Reynolds. With her inherent sense of the past, the Queen likes to point out that West's charming portrait of Queen Charlotte and her thirteen children was George III's special favourite and hung in his breakfast-room in Buckingham House. Two other favourites, until recently, were the two great Gainsboroughs, the superb full-length portrait of Colonel Leger, institutor of the classic race, and the portrait of John Fischer, hautboy player, in his plum-coloured coat and breeches, the Court musician who married Gainsborough's daughter. But the Queen characteristically insisted that they should have a wider audience and they were recently seen in the State Rooms open to the public at Windsor Castle.

The Palace Picture Gallery often engages the attention of guests after dinner. In King George V's reign the pictures were still stacked, here and there, four high on the damask walls. The Queen has simplified this distracting pattern, dispatching the least important paintings elsewhere by the dozen. *Rembrandt and Saskia* hangs in enhanced dignity, no longer overtopped by a stormy Van der Velde. With the pictures hung at eye-level, the braggadocio of Frans Hals's *Young Man* has free space and Van Dyck's *Study of Horsemen* and the mighty Rubens composition of *St. George and the Dragon* can each produce their persuasions uninterrupted. The Queen likes to tell how her shining Vermeer *The Music Lesson* was once so wisely admired by Queen Charlotte in its days of nonentity that it hung in her dressing-room. There are stories also in *Charles I, the Queen and her Dwarf, Jeffery Hudson* by Daniel Mytens, for the group includes the original Tom Thumb who stepped from a pie and yet lived to be of account to the secret service. There is the tiny Watteau canvas *La Surprise*, which surprises most people in its size; and the remarkable Ruysdael *The Windmill*, its sunset and storm awakening sensations of awe, though the painter died destitute. Not that the Queen regales her guests solely with anecdote. Hostess in her own home, she regards her pictures with affection tempered with pride and yet is anxious that others should share her enjoyment.

When the Queen is abroad and left to her own devices she often elects to visit an art gallery. Thus, when the Queen and the Duke of Edinburgh visited Amsterdam for Queen Juliana's silver wedding celebrations, they rose early one morning to snatch the opportunity to revisit the Rijksmuseum. Her Majesty had first visited the "Rijks" during her State visit to the

Netherlands in 1958, but now she clearly wished to improve her first impressions and study the presentation and even showmanship for which the Rijksmuseum is celebrated. Rembrandt's masterpiece *The Night Watch* has a room to itself. Would it be possible, or even desirable, to display any one of the Queen's pictures alone? What is the best spacing or context of the cabinet pictures of Jan Steen and Teniers? According to the Press, Dr. Van Schendel, the Rijksmuseum's director, was astounded at the Queen's knowledge of Dutch painters.

But we also have expert authority that the Queen's collection of Dutch and Flemish masterpieces is itself probably unexampled throughout the world. Sir Anthony Blunt has asserted of the Buckingham Palace pictures that nowhere else can Cuyp and Teniers be seen in such varied perfection. The Queen possesses ten notable paintings by Cuyp, eighteen by Teniers, eight Jan Steens of the finest quality and two of the most brilliant works of Pieter de Hooch, besides Gerard Dou, Gabriel Metsu and others in rich profusion. Although mere names and titles can be tedious, attention has often been drawn to Jan Steen's *The Morning Toilet*, its exquisite colour paramount in the hyacinth-blue of the bed hangings; *The Letter* by Ter Borch, and all the little subject pictures: *This House for Sale* by Van Ostade, with the bailiff's men seemingly in possession; *The Listening Housewife* by Nicolas Maes, in which a young woman steals down a staircase, conspiratorial finger to lip; the crowded dancing scene of Teniers's *Village Festival* and the farming paintings of Paul Potter. Some of these pictures are so small that fifty were once displayed in a single room at the Royal Academy. Gerard Dou's *Maidservant Cleaning a Pan* contains a world of innocent reflection on a pearwood panel not six inches wide. The Wouvermans and Van Meiris and other "little masters" might have been painted to suit the modern taste for small pictures.

The Queen's artistic training, which began with that regular sustained study of a picture a week in her schooldays, can be seen in maturity in her alert knowledge and care of all the paintings at Buckingham Palace. One might readily expect the Queen's pictures to be maintained in singularly perfect condition, and thirty years of meticulous attention have been further accorded them since Clifford Smith found them "notably free from the too prevalent fault of over-varnishing". In the great cleaning controversy the Queen is on the side of new judgments and practically every royal picture of consequence has been cleaned since the war.

III

It has been neatly said that the paintings at Buckingham Palace and Windsor Castle can be compared with burgundy and claret. At the Palace the solid merits of the Dutch school impart a body and foundation, while at Windsor there is more light and gaiety. In the same terms Hampton Court is the vintage port of the Crown collection, old and crusted, too heavy for the average palate and too long in the cellar. Without taking the simile farther, Windsor Castle affords both greater publicity and deeper privacy. By the Queen's express wish, tourists throng murmurously through the State Rooms for the greater part of the year, free to admire many of her finest paintings, some only recently transferred from Buckingham Palace, while in the private apartments the Queen can share her leisured enjoyments with her friends.

It was at Windsor, during the Ascot week house-party in 1961, that she first showed her guests her new contemporary paintings. The arts thus follow the light relaxation of the races.

In the Castle, with its memories of Charles II and the later Georges, as at the Palace, the Queen likes to take newcomers round and show them her treasures. Guests have told how interestingly and knowledgeably she recounts the history of the paintings and furniture; and the tour, occupying much of the evening, itself connotes the changed Windsor atmosphere. Lady Diana Cooper amusingly described her first experience as a guest early in King George VI's reign, her sitting-room and bedroom stuffed with twenty-two oil paintings of royalty, her bathroom replete with another eight oil paintings and two bronze statuettes. A present-day guest suite has pale walls adorned only by a modern painting or two, with contemporary furniture that is simple and comfortable yet elegant and refreshing.

When closed to the public, the State Apartments are not omitted from the tours of inspection. I have been told how vigilantly the Queen supervises the appearance and well-being of this Charles II suite, from inconspicuous improvements in lighting to the tactful touches of arrangement and floral decoration that diminish — except perhaps in crowded August — the museum atmosphere. The King's Withdrawing Room was long known as the Rubens Room, for instance, but the Queen prefers to restore the old names. Now the walls have been hung with fresh damask, the ornate ceiling simplified by plainer paintwork, and a sense of space regained by evicting the opulent overstaffed armchairs and cluttering side-tables, and giving the remaining suite new pine-green upholstery. The eleven paintings on the walls have been reduced to six, chiefly by removing the spurious pictures that the enlightened long knew were not the work of Rubens at all. There are now the great *Summer* and *Winter Scenes*, *The Holy Family*, the celebrated *Family of Sir Balthasar Gerbier*, besides the unascribed equestrian portrait of Philip of Spain and *St. Martin Dividing His Cloak*, now known to be by Van Dyck. The State Bedroom, too, has had its profusion of pictures reduced to three or four, and the portrait of Bridget Holmes with her broom, a serving woman at the court of King Charles, has been, most aptly, removed to the back stairs. Gainsborough's hautboy was tried here for a time, but when I last visited the room the pictures were still "in course of rearrangement". So also was the furniture, with the more appropriate pieces taking pride of established position. The bed bears the initials of the Emperor Louis Napoleon and the Queen fittingly decided that the Aubusson carpet presented to her by General de Gaulle in 1960 should be its companion.

Similar changes can be found throughout the State Rooms. You may still see the Holbeins in the Queen's Withdrawing Room — the former Picture Gallery — but now there are some twenty-four aptly arranged canvases where no fewer than fifty-eight were formerly crowded together. Castle veterans who have never before seen so many variations admire this policy of freshness. The Queen's Closet was formerly an expanse of Canalettos, and nothing else, but the Queen dislikes sterile classification and has introduced Hoppner, Reynolds, and Gainsborough to lend variety. The Queen's Ballroom, formerly known as the Van Dyck Room, remains unchanged in its beauty and harmony, though given new counterpoint by a Canaletto and other newcomers, and in King Charles II's Dining Room the unaccustomed eye will not notice the floodlights, concealed in bowls on carved pedestals, that finely illuminate the feasting gods of Verrio's ceiling.

Only three of the twenty sumptuous ceilings originally painted at Windsor by Antonio Verrio in 1678–80 survive today, and all three can at last be admired with adequate lighting. One can imagine the Queen's active concern and even dismay when water from a broken rainwater pipe seeped through the Italian's original work in the Queen's Audience Chamber. The central figure in her swan-drawn chariot of Queen Catherine of Braganza was almost obliterated and about a quarter of the remaining painted surface seriously stained and undermined. Fortunately the Ministry of Works was able to more than "make good" the damage. Their highly skilled restorer, Mr. J. E. Meade, resorted to photographs to show what had been lost in the scarred and cloudy firmament and not only reconstructed the damaged area, using Verrio's method of building up colour in thin glazes, but also removed a false and misleading restoration of William IV's reign. In little more than a year Queen Catherine could not only be seen again but the ceiling was better than ever.

Queen Elizabeth, however, commanded a systematic inspection to guard against any future water damage. It is a wise monarch who keeps her Minister of Works up to scratch and the present reign has seen a continuous and notable programme of repair and improvement at Windsor Castle. The fastidious may quarrel with over-bright bricks used to repair the red chimneys of the Horseshoe Cloister, but even the Queen is dependent upon her architects and the resource of suppliers. In essence necessary modernity throughout the Castle has always paid respect to the old, and the Queen has properly limited, without destroying, the tributes to the fabric made by Queen Victoria and King Edward VII. Queen Victoria would recognize her Audience Room even to carpets and colouring, and only the overmantels and door-headings have been simplified. The chamber in the Clarence Tower in which George IV, William IV, and the Prince Consort all died is no longer funereal in appearance. Walls and door alike are painted a delicate green with plinths and panelling picked out

in gold. Far from being too vivid in mournful reminder, a gay
Munnings painting hangs over the fireplace, the picture of the
Ascot ride which delighted King George V because he could
recognize the grooms, a pleasure of meticulous painting which
the Queen herself shared as a child.

Few portraits of the present reign have supplanted their
predecessors. In the private apartments the Beechey portraits
of George III's daughters still claim as their rightful home, the
Crimson Drawing Room, though Sir Gerald Kelly's state
portraits of George VI and his Consort hold the place of
honour with the majestic furniture from Carlton House. In the
Green Drawing Room Lawrence's *Princess Sophia* — one of the
twenty pictures which the Queen loaned to the Royal
Academy's Lawrence exhibition — has been reinstated in regal
splendour against the green damask walls. In the White
Drawing Room is perhaps the finest piece of furniture in all
the royal palaces, the richly embellished cabinet of comte
d'Artois, afterwards Charles X of France, in company with the
delightful Hoppner princesses. It was with one of these that
King George VI used to enjoy pointing out a family likeness he
saw in Princess Margaret. Nowadays, in the Queen's sitting-
room, some visitors imagine a resemblance to Queen Elizabeth
II in Francis Cotes's portrait of Queen Charlotte with her
plump and amusing baby. The Queen herself at all events is
fond of this charming, maternal study, and enjoys pointing out
the baby, grown to womanhood, in a nearby Gainsborough
portrait. With this work, indeed, Francis Cotes as a founder
member of the Royal Academy, is placed in the company of
the Queen's finest Gainsboroughs, but the painter of the
draperies which lend such style to Cotes's pictures is
posthumously honoured with still greater point. Mr. Toms,
R.A., was a specialist who charged twenty guineas for adding

the realistic effects of curtains and costume, but the early death of his chief patron unnerved him and he took to drink and committed suicide. He might have stayed his hand had he known that, nearly two centuries later, the flowers in the Queen's sitting-room would always be carefully matched against his painted draperies.

Sharing by proxy in the Queen's hospitality at Windsor, we may also admire the little group of four *fête-galant* scenes by Pater, which were fond favourites of the Queen Mother. The most varied array of all the Queen's pictures, however, has been deliberately and effectively stage-managed for her guests in the magnificent green-carpeted Grand Corridor that runs for 550 feet around the Castle quadrangle; "such a place for a walky-walky", as Creevey once said. Thanks to Wyatville's deliberate plan, the corridor links all the private apartments, yet less than one-third of its length meets the eye at a time.

Whether the exploring glance looks east or south, one is confronted at each turn with novelty. Here is the amusing picture which Hieronymus Janssens painted of a youthful Charles II pointing his toes in a gavotte at a ball at the Hague; here are portraits by Reynolds and Lawrence — including Lawrence's *Sir Walter Scott* — here are the decorative landscapes of Zuccarelli, added to Canaletto, with Zoffany's *Tribuna of the Uffizi* and his *Lapidaries*. Or at least here they are part of the time, loans and frequent changes permitting. Hogarth's portrait of *David Garrick and his Wife* may be here, I am enigmatically reminded, when it is not elsewhere, and it was to be publicly seen in the State Apartments in 1962. The Corridor also boasts the portrait of Garrick by Reynolds and beneath it there usually hangs Zoffany's portrait of Queen Charlotte and her two eldest children, recently seen at the Queen's Gallery. In the picture a waisted longcase clock of distinctive shape can be seen and now the identical clock, or its sister, usually keeps the portrait company.

This picture was also loaned to the exhibition of eighteenth-century painting at the Royal Academy when Professor Albert Richardson had just become President and still new to his tasks. When the Queen visited the exhibition and he conducted her round, he had intended to tell Her Majesty about each picture, but indeed, as he said, "She told me, and I did nearly all the listening. She amazed me. She discussed the compositions and talked about the derivation of the exhibits. I could not add to her knowledge."

Pausing before the Zoffany portrait, the Professor hoped to remind the Queen of the tradition that the room was in old Buckingham House. "Or was it Windsor — or perhaps Kew Palace?" the Queen asked, smilingly. "The 1816 Carlton House catalogue calls it an apartment at Windsor. The clock was there in Queen Charlotte's time. It was one of a pair and they are still there, you know."

The Queen was amused, rather than dogmatic. Having started the hare of a perplexing mystery, she caused inquiries to be made and the room was more certainly identified as one in Kew Palace. Professor Richardson said with admiration afterwards that one would have to go back to George III to find a reigning monarch to equal her knowledge. As for us, the story rings now with insight. We have studied the founding and the growth of the Queen's intimate and complex understanding of her pictures, and can recognize that the Crown collection has a worthy chatelaine.

IV

Sandringham House and Balmoral Castle are, of course, the private homes of the Queen and the paintings are similarly private in character. At Sandringham, however, the Queen likes to make use of the Commonwealth gifts that can grace the background of her everyday life, and thus the privileged visitor may find Manly MacDonald's picture of the Toronto skyline and Robert Pilot's view of the Ottawa Parliament Buildings oddly catching the light of the Norfolk countryside. Canadians are apt to decry their native art, but the Queen values a characteristic Cranberry Lake study by Fred Haines, R.C.A., and she owns four or five pictures by A. Y. Jackson and other original members of the Group of Seven. Australian art, similarly, claims regard in her private life: apart from the symbolic Philpot presentation piece *Apotheosis of the British* the Queen also owns such works as *The Opossum and the Moon* by Bryan Marshall, the landscape *Heavitree Gap* by Albert Namatjira and two views, such as the Queen saw for herself from Government House, Sydney, by Rubery Bennett and Jean Ramsay. Such pictures also have a place of sentiment, not entirely unlike that accorded the painting of the Queen's Coronation bouquet of white flowers, which Anne Zinkeisen painted in her studio while the flowers were still fresh and then gave to the Queen.

Except for a collection of miniatures, Sandringham House was not notable for its art in former days. The family groups in the saloon, the lurid Spanish tapestries in the dining-room and a large oil painting of Edward VII with blazing gun on a tiger-hunt, all these embalmed a period while petrifying artistic sensibilities. The Queen had to visit the art gallery at Port Sunlight to become better acquainted with the Pre-Raphaelites. Sandringham has an admirable collection of sketches dating from John Leech through Phil May to Giles and the modern cartoons from the Clarence House corridor, but until the turn of the century a Landseer self-portrait — with dogs —

probably remained the mansion's chief art treasure. It is a matter for regret that Landseer died soon after the paintwork of Sandringham itself was dry, and so Norfolk worthies were not preserved for us in the manner of the remarkable series of pastels of Highland gillies and keepers in the dining-room at Balmoral Castle.

It may occasion surprise that the remarkable profusion of Landseer dogs and landscapes at the Queen's Scottish home has not been noticeably modified with the passage of time. The Queen Mother dids not subject many modern paintings to the climatic hazards of neighbouring Birkhall and the Castle of Mey; Stuart prints were apt to be more in evidence and no doubt this sufficiently indicates the Queen's own attitude to Balmoral. But Sandringham has been successively made over by Queen Mary, Queen Elizabeth the Queen Mother, and now by the Queen herself. It is rightly the home of the Munnings painting of *Aureole*, of Lynwood Palmer's evocation of *The Tetrarch*, and other equine studies. On the other hand, the bronze statuette of Aureole by Herbert Haseltine, the American sculptor, remains in London. Lionel Hamilton-Renwick also painted the Queen's champion thoroughbred, and when he wanted to borrow his picture for an exhibition he had merely to go to Buckingham Palace, where Prince Philip personally handed it over and admonished him "Don't forget to bring it back".

To all accounts however, the Queen also likes to have a few of her lesser Dutch paintings at Sandringham, where the selection is changed from time to time, a sure mark of actual interest. Prince Philip also has a Marc Chagall picture given to him when he met the artist in Denmark; there are one or two gifts by modern Swedish artists, including Titus Wikstrom, and such gifts at various times already amount to a small and reasonably representative modern collection in the Queen's country home. Not least, it is interesting to note that the tradesmen holding Royal Warrants of Appointment to the Queen or to the Duke of Edinburgh included firms of picture restorers and repairers, three picture-frame makers, three groups specializing in fine art photography and a firm styled as "packers of Works of Art". On a royal scale, the fine arts require careful housekeeping.

5: THE ARTS AND THE COURT

I

The Queen rules her territories as a supreme act of government at the wish of her diverse peoples. Her Court is the nucleus of an ancient and emotional idea, first expressed in terms of warrior leadership, and yet a shadow court of culture has been intrinsic in the Court of State for eight hundred years. The Plantagenets were encouraging art, music, poetry and architecture when they were laying the stones of Windsor. Henry II rewarded the stanzas of his King's Versifier with an annual two tuns of wine; Richard II left the impress of his age in the Wilton Diptych; Henry VII exchanged the Order of the Garter for Raphael's *St. George*. Holbein's most brilliant years were spent as Court Painter to Henry VIII and the arts of the Tudor age were expressed in the architecture and furniture of a profusion of palaces.

The first Queen Elizabeth appointed Nicholas Hilliard her official Limner or Miniature Painter and Edmund Spenser earned £100, which may be reckoned £2,000 by today's standards, by reading his *Faerie Queen* before the Queen as a serial. It was Ben Jonson who wrote and presented some of the masques at the Court of King James I; and Charles I, as we know, had his agents scouring Europe for paintings, persuaded Rubens to design the ceilings of his palace in Whitehall, and provided Van Dyck with a house and a pension. He had, too, a Herald painter whose task was to illuminate letters to such rulers as "the Emperor and Patriarch of Russia, the Grand Signor, the Great Mogul, the Emperor of Persia … and other far-distant kings". Such posts multiplied. Dryden was the first

86

poet to receive the title of Poet Laureate or King's Orator by letters patent; Robert Streater was Sergeant Painter; and a Portrait Painter, a Limner, a Master of the Musick, and a Master of the Revels were soon all found on the payroll.

To examine more modern times, Queen Victoria included Southey, Wordsworth, Tennyson, and Alfred Austin among her Poets Laureate; James Sant was Painter in Ordinary, Joseph Boehm was dubbed Queen's Sculptor and Oswald Brierley was appointed under the Lord Chamberlain as Marine Painter. We need not pause to inquire into vanished reputations. There were also both English and German Librarians, a Surveyor of Pictures, and a Scottish Historiographer, although the Scottish posting of Painter and Limner had been allowed to fall into abeyance. Under the renewals of Edward VII's reign, a sturdier school took charge and Sir Lionel Cust, Director of the National Portrait Gallery, was appointed Surveyor of the King's Pictures and Works of Art, *vide* the warrant of appointment, to usher in an era of revived care and scholarship. Francis Laking, Christie's foremost authority on armour, was installed in the new post of Keeper of the King's Armoury. Presently King George V appointed Sir Edward Elgar as Master of the King's Musick, and John Masefield became Poet Laureate.

The true origin of these royal artistic postings are nearly lost in musty records, but they remain grouped, as they have been for centuries, under the Lord Chamberlain as titular head of the Queen's Household. With some exceptions, they tend increasingly to be onerous and hard-working occupations rather than honorary sinecures. It seems appropriate that they should be quartered in St. James's Palace, for the "Court of St. James's" remains the titular Court of the Sovereign in official diplomacy. Save for the aegis of the Lord Chamberlain, the

Queen's artistic household enjoys no separate existence. It is not to be found listed in the handbooks as resoundingly as the Queen's Ecclesiastical Household, for example, or even the Medical Household. Yet the atmosphere of any Court is to a great extent the imprint of its age; the Queen's cultural Court is a reality, and it has become a department of sustained expertise.

Thus the Surveyor of the Queen's Pictures, Sir Anthony Frederick Blunt, K.C.V.O., was the Director of the Courtauld Institute of Art, the leading venue of scientific art inquiry in London, as well as Professor of History of Art of London University. At Cambridge he read mathematics, but as a man of 30 he joined the staff of the Warburg Institute, with its concern for the survival of classical ideals, and his first book, *Artistic Theory in Italy*, published in 1940 when he was 33, illustrated the breadth both of his knowledge and authority. He subsequently published studies of Nicholas Poussin and of the art of William Blake; his book *Art and Architecture in France* appeared in Coronation Year, and he devoted himself to a series of complete and detailed accounts of the various collections of drawings at Windsor Castle, the French drawings and the Venetian, the Roman drawings, the work of Castiglione and so forth, which wase followed by a six-volume catalogue of the complete Crown paintings. This learned, absorbed, brilliant man was the Queen's chief artistic adviser. On matters of policy or doubt in regard to art, Sir Anthony Blunt was consulted and Her Majesty closely considered his advice.

The Queen, however, gives her approval to the appointment or reappointment of members of the Royal Fine Art Commission only in consultation with her Private Secretary. A Royal Warrant since the war has implemented the

Commission's Terms of Reference with considerable power: "We do give and grant unto you … full power to call before you any such persons as you shall judge likely to afford you any information … and also to call for, have access to and examine all books, documents, registers and records…" The presence on the Commission of personalities with whom the Sovereign is in more or less regular contact also enables the Queen to make her views known on points of controversy. King George VI, for instance, speedily disposed of Giles Scott's proposed design for the interior of Coventry Cathedral, when he was shown it at the Royal Academy. "It looks like an air-raid shelter," he said, testily, and as a former secretary of the Royal Fine Arts Commission has testified, this was one of the reasons why the Scott design was unacceptable.

In contrast, Mr. Oliver Millar, M.V.O., F.S.A., Deputy Surveyor of the Queen's Paintings, was concerned chiefly with the day-to-day administration of the Crown collection of paintings; with the maintenance and arrangement and the thousand-and-one problems involved in tending a great art collection. He similarly was professionally trained for his career at the Courtauld Institute and gained the University of London's Academic Diploma in the history of art; and he has written books and monographs on Gainsborough and William Dobson and on English art in the seventeenth century: an enthusiast, one may rank him, whose attainments and life's work were happily matched. In his book-lined sanctum at the top of the magnificent stairway of St. James's Palace, he devoted himself to a systematic study of the history of the royal collection. He published a new edition of the catalogue of Charles I's collection, and was general editor, with Sir Anthony, of the new *catalogue raisonné* of the Queen's pictures.

The Queen takes pride and pleasure in thus dispensing practical help in the scholarship of the fine arts. The Crown collection is unique in its long traditions and few of the world's great hoards of art are so firmly founded on thorough documentation and scientific analysis. An early French still life, a study of a bowl of flowers, was catalogued for the saleroom as signed and dated by the artist, Louise Moillon, 1634, for example, but Mr. Millar was able to identify the work as a far rarer treasure, a lost picture from the collection of King Charles I. Against such romantic episodes, time also has to be spent in organizing the loan of royal pictures. The Queen is "extremely generous", to quote Mr. Millar, in allowing her pictures and other works of art to be seen by others. Over a thousand loans have been made within ten years, but, apart from a few guiding axioms, Her Majesty's consent is sought and notified for every individual exhibition. When a picture is loaned "by gracious permission of H.M. The Queen" the phrase does not cloak an automatic action undertaken by an assistant private secretary: Her Majesty has, in fact, personally considered the loan and approved it. Visiting the Mellon Gallery in Washington during her 1957 American tour, she was not surprised to find several Blake drawings on loan from Windsor Castle. She already knew precisely which ones had been lent and showed herself acquainted with the precautions taken to ensure their safe transit across the Atlantic.

Royal pictures in the present reign have been dispersed as widely as Brussels, Venice, Rome, Cape Town, and Melbourne. In 1961, when the Windsor State Apartments were undergoing redecoration and overhaul, forty-seven of the finest paintings were loaned to the National Museum of Wales and the National Gallery of Scotland, a royal gesture of trust and confidence that was without parallel. With four Rembrandts, six Rubens and thirteen Van Dycks, the insurance cover of £750,000 for theft in transit represented only a marginal hazard. The Queen's desire to share her pictures must necessarily be balanced against the vulnerability of a fragile work of art. The Queen's famous Negress Head clock was lent to an exhibition in Paris and, upset by travel, has never told the time so smoothly since. Climatic hazards abroad must clearly entail a regretful refusal, although risks can occur even close to home. When the foremost art dealers of eight nations staged their International Art Treasures Exhibition at the Victoria and Albert Museum in 1962, the Queen paid a private visit, attracted by a display that ranged from magnificent furniture to Georgian silver, English and continental porcelain and oriental ceramics. The news of her interest thereupon lured so many people that the heat they engendered, crowded under the bright lights, is said to have occasioned splits and damage of the delicate veneers and casing of some of the exhibits, including a medal cabinet made by William Vile for George III, not in the royal collection.

This was an exhibition, one imagines, that Queen Mary would not have missed, and Queen Elizabeth elected to be accompanied both by Sir Anthony Blunt and Sir James Mann, then Surveyor of the Queen's Works of Art. We have recognized that the Queen's attitude to the fine arts is not superficial: it is, indeed, one of close attention and even authority, but the Queen assesses her own knowledge at a modest level and this was an occasion when she wished to be expertly informed. Sir James Mann died in 1962 after devoting sixteen years to maintaining the furnishings of the Crown collection, from the Paris-made throne of Edward VII, the one now used by the Queen on suitable occasions, to the porcelain, bibelots, clocks and barometers throughout the royal palaces.

His field of interest was both wider and narrower than that of the Surveyor of the Queen's Pictures, for he was concerned with the furniture of Buckingham Palace and Windsor Castle, but not the maintenance of the pieces in the state rooms of St. James's Palace nor the historic furniture and tapestries of Hampton Court, Kensington Palace, Kew Palace, and Holyroodhouse, which are the separate responsibility of the Ministry of Works. Like Sir Anthony Blunt, Sir James Mann was not required to allot all his time to the royal treasures. He was also Director of the Wallace Collection, chairman of the National Buildings Record and a vice-president of the Society of Antiquaries. He also was once Deputy Director of the Courtauld Institute and a Reader in the History of Art at London University, but he began his career as assistant keeper of fine art at the Ashmolean Museum before becoming an assistant to the Keeper of the Wallace Collection at the age of 27. As one might expect, he was a specialist in armour, French sculpture and church sculpture; and the Queen's collection of armour ranges from the finer pieces of King Henry VIII's arsenal to the Japanese sword ceremoniously surrendered by Field-Marshal Terauchi to Earl Mountbatten in 1945.

Here, again, when the Queen lends pieces of furniture, china, sculpture or bibelots for exhibition — and she loaned no fewer than fourteen Regency pieces from Buckingham Palace for the bicentenary exhibition at the Brighton Pavilion in 1962 — the details were arranged by Mr. Francis Watson, M.V.O., F.S.A., who began his Court career under the late Sir James's tutelage, and although his duties lay nominally with the Crown, they also overlapped into the Queen's private interests. Thus Queen Mary privately owned two imitation bamboo cabinets which had been modernized by the disguise of blue and gold paint. The Queen returned them through Mr. Watson as a gift to the

Pavilion, where, with the paint removed, they have been restored to their original appearance. Similarly, in 1961–2, the Queen lent a number of fascinating objects from the royal collections to the Exhibition of Royal Gifts at Christie's in aid of the Y.W.C.A., and Mr. Watson had the task of selecting the objects of best interest, from the shirt worn by Charles I at his execution to the table of victory which was ordered by Napoleon to celebrate his military prowess, but left forgotten at the Sèvres factory after the battle of Waterloo.

The loan of any one of the Queen's five hundred Leonardo drawings, on the other hand, involves Miss Aydua Scott-Elliot, M.V.O., as Keeper of the Prints and Drawings at Windsor, a title devised at the Queen's wish to give a more precise posting than "Assistant to the Librarian". The growth in the official staff of the Royal Library is noteworthy. Only Sir Owen Morshead was listed as Librarian in the days when King George V summoned him from time to time to discuss the books the King hoped to read or had been reading. In the present reign, in addition to the Librarian, Mr. R. C. Mackworth-Young, and his assistant, Miss Hedley, a Household Appointment was also enjoyed by Sir John Wheeler-Bennett, K.C.V.O., C.M.G., as Historical Adviser to the Royal Archives, a position of the highest trust and responsibility for the man who was at Gordonstoun with Prince Philip and so ably prepared the official biography of King George VI.

Then there were the lighter duties of Sir Arthur Bliss as Master of the Queen's Music. The final, archaic "k" of "Musick" was quietly dropped during Sir Edgar Elgar's service in this role to King George V, and it was only owing to Elgar's acute representations, earlier in the reign, that the whole office was not dropped at all. It had, in fact, been scheduled for suppression, until Elgar wrote urgently to Lord Stamfordham, the King's Secretary, protesting that the effacement of "the last shred of connexion of the Court to Art" would not be understood abroad. There was no reply. "No reply, *no grit*, no imagination, no *music*. No nothing except boxing, football, racing..." the old lion roared, and he waxed indignant that George V wanted little but *Land of Hope and Glory* at the opening of the British Empire Exhibition. But Elgar was mistaken, as others have been; he was appointed at an emolument of £100 a year and launched himself energetically in putting the royal collection of musical instruments in good order. His *Nursery Suite* of 1931 was dedicated to the then Princess Elizabeth and Princess Margaret.

We need not assume that Sir Arthur Bliss concerned himself with the military band music at royal garden parties and State dinners, but he wrote a Processional for the Coronation (though his predecessor, Sir Arnold Bax, had the honour of composing the Coronation March); he advised the Queen on musical appointments and honours, kept her informed of changes in the constitution of Royal Philharmonic Society and similar bodies, and also had the nominal responsibility of the high musical merit of the choirs of the Chapels Royal, a task he in reality deferred to W. H. Gabb, F.R.C.O., the appointed "Organist, Choirmaster and Composer". In Elgar's day, royal visits to concerts were so infrequent that the Master of Music was called on to make all the arrangements and be in attendance for private presentations, but the present Queen attends concerts, the ballet or the opera, with such comparative frequency and informality that arrangements are quietly settled through a secretary. Sir Arthur Bliss advised the Queen in the composite Royal Charter that inaugurated the combined ballet forces of Covent Garden and Sadler's Wells as the Royal Ballet, and he was consulted in all matters involving the service of music in ceremonial. The position of Poet Laureate is similarly not treated by its holder as a sinecure. Although it may now offer only £72 a year, with a perquisite of £27 in lieu of the traditional butt of sack, John Masefield performed the service with great integrity, supplying verses not only for coronations and weddings but such occasions as royal births and homecomings. He also headed the committee which annually advised Her Majesty on the award of the Queen's Poetry Medal. The artistic appointments of the Queen's Scottish Household were similarly maintained with Stanley Cursiter, C.B.E., R.S.A., as Painter and Limner, and Sir William Reid Dick, K.C.V.O., as sculptor.

The theatrical duties of the Lord Chamberlain make him always a popular butt and, in considering the cultural offices of the Court, we may not ignore nor need we look askance at the four Examiners of Plays — one being a parson appointed to examine plays in Welsh — who also officially operate within the Royal Household under the Lord Chamberlain's direct aegis. Is it a paradox that the Queen, though constantly proving herself an enthusiastic patron of the theatre, should also employ a quartet of officials who act as play censors and thus curtail the freedom of expression of the stage?

A Court point of view is that this is the nub of one of the deepest-grained fallacies that surround and distort our ideas of the royal prerogative. The Examiners regard their function as protective rather than restrictive, and essentially well disposed rather than inimical. Their inherent policies stem from the days of Shakespeare's boyhood, when the Puritans of the City of London denounced the traffic of the playhouse, including the university dramatists, and the Lord Chamberlain with other peers was thereupon empowered to safeguard the status of all players by licence. Elizabeth I maintained her own company of players, in royal livery, closely controlled by the Master of the Revels, eight years before Shakespeare wrote his first play. We find James I granting a royal licence to Shakespeare's company in 1603 "freely to use and exercise the art and faculty of playing comedies, tragedies, histories, interludes, morals, pastorals, stage plays and such like … as well for the recreation of our loving subjects as for our solace and pleasure…" In 1737 Henry Fielding's dramatic satires were politically so corrosive that Parliament passed its Licensing Act "to restrain the political and personal satire … which the Government found embarrassing", and a power of veto was conferred on the Lord Chamberlain as an impartial figure who could occupy the judgment seat while embodying the non-political, non-controversial and high moral and academic qualities of the Crown. "A very invidious post," Lord Chesterfield observed, "to be obliged by his office to be the standard of wit, politeness and good sense to the whole nation."

A slight shift in the Lord Chamberlain's fiat came in 1843, when the Theatres Act authorized him to ban any stage play which he considered to be contrary to "good manners, decorum and the preservation of the public peace". Hence his powers still stem more fully from Parliament than from the Queen. In 1949 a Censorship of Plays (Repeal) Bill reached its second reading in the House of Commons, finally failing, however, under the heavy guns of the Theatres National Committee, which represented the theatre managers themselves. When it came to the point, the theatres recognized the useful services of the Lord Chamberlain and preferred his regulated hazards to the chaos that might have resulted from an infinity of bans and codes imposed by police and local authorities. The refusal of the Lord Chamberlain's licence does not prevent a play from being performed, for it can still be staged before the members of a private theatre club. The issue of a licence, however, places dramatists, producers and players under the protection of the Crown; and the prescribed reading fee of two guineas is thus the negligible premium of an insurance against prosecution, provided one does not wildly flout the rules of local justices in "ensuring decency".

The Lord Chamberlain's fee has not changed for years, but the Play Examiners of every reign tended to reflect the mores of their time. Critics of the stage censorship today generally have to hark back to *Mrs. Warren's Profession* or Ibsen's *Ghosts* to make an effective point, and we cannot blame the Queen's present servants for the judgments — perhaps even the mistakes, conditioned by the climate of thought — of their predecessors. Some newspapers found *The Merry Widow* the most improper and immoral play that had ever been produced, as George Edwardes once admitted, but it was given a licence. The censorship of the present reign has in the event already demonstrated a wider vision and good sense than the managements themselves. The performance of *Lady Chatterley's Lover* in the theatre seemed as absurd and disconcerting as it might have been if read to a graduation class, and the replacement of the Shavian adjective by a four-letter dockyard synonym in *My Fair Lady* was a *coup d'theatre* sufficiently ineffective and tasteless to make Bernard Shaw turn in his grave.

It was once claimed in committee evidence that a licence had been refused only to twenty out of 4,233 plays submitted and any reasonable examination of present-day censorship extinguishes charges of despotism. The kiss between two men caused the proscription of Arthur Miller's *A View from the Bridge*; the homosexual fears of the hero incurred the ban of

Robert Anderson's *Tea and Sympathy*, but both plays were, in the event, "privately" shown to large audiences. It is difficult to see how the Lord Chamberlain could have passed the large number of "four-letter words" in Genet's *The Balcony* while observing his mandate for "good manners and decorum". Cuts were requested in Lionel Bart's *Fings…* only after complaints had suggested their wisdom. Good taste could have been invoked, more than the protocol against the representation of members of the Royal Family, in the case of an Ionesco playlet upon the Duke and Duchess of Windsor. One has to return to 1951 and a previous reign for the absurdity of a ban — on the grounds of historical inaccuracy — on an operetta concerned with Victoria and Albert. Against these issues one sets the liberty accorded the new playwrights of the Royal Court Theatre and their allies. The Lord Chamberlain dexterously avoided the catcalls that might have arisen had he forbidden the girl dancers of the Ballets Africains from being bare above the waist. Centuries of draped tradition were set aside by the document of licence — which Shaw earlier found so "insolent and insufferable" — that the ballet did not "in its general tendency … contain anything improper for the stage".

Apart from the unpopular and misunderstood duties of censorship, the Lord Chamberlain is also responsible for licensing the theatres at which a monarch might be expected to seek enjoyment; for example, within the parliamentary boundaries of London and Westminster and in the old boroughs of Finsbury, Marylebone, Tower Hamlets, Lambeth, Southwark, Brighton, and Windsor. When Queen Elizabeth II takes the guests of her Ascot house-party to watch the repertory players at the Theatre Royal, Windsor, she is closer than we perhaps suspect to Queen Elizabeth I.

"...by the Grace of God... Queen, Head of the Commonwealth, Defender of the Faith, Sovereign of the British Orders of Knighthood, Captain General of the Royal Regiment of Artillery and the Honourable Artillery Company, Colonel-in-Chief of the Life Guards..." So the sonorous phrases of the Queen's titles roll on, until we find her "Head of the Civil Defence Corps, Head of the National Hospital Service Reserve." For the sake of the balanced view it may be held regrettable that the resounding list does not go on to include Her Majesty's sovereign positions in the artistic Establishment, commencing with her role as Patron, Protector and Supporter of the Royal Academy of Arts. Nevertheless this is a function which the Queen upholds as dutifully and conscientiously as if it had been implicit in the "princely virtues" of her Coronation prayers. It was highly apposite and no accident that the first public function the Queen elected to attend in her Coronation year was a dinner given to her by the Royal Academy, and every Royal Academician contributed to a bound portfolio of watercolours and drawings which formed a prized and praiseworthy gift among the avalanche of Coronation presentations.

When George III approved the founding of the Royal Academy in 1768, extending a charter he had granted to the "Incorporated Society of Artists" four years earlier, he established its school in the then royal palace of Somerset House, subsequently cleared the Society's £5,000 debts and, with some insight of the artistic temperament, he debated and drew up its title deeds, the Instrument of Establishment, with great care and deliberation lest Academicians should find cause to quarrel. The Twenty-seven Articles even laid down that there should be a porter and sweeper, and stipulated the salaries of these lowly servants of the arts. Henceforward the King always called the institution "my Academy". For the Queen it is similarly her Academy. Any amendment of the laws requires her assent, and when Academicians have elected or re-elected their President they may not leave the meeting until the Queen's agreement has been obtained. The interval is less protracted than of yore, now that the matter is settled by telephone with the Keeper of the Privy Purse, but the principle of the royal prerogative remains. When Sir Albert Richardson was re-elected President for a year as an exception beyond the normal retiring age of 75, the Queen had specially to sanction his re-election, and when it was decided to curb the drain on Academy funds by imposing a handling fee of 10$s.$ on the work of would-be summer exhibitors — the first charge ever imposed upon artists — the matter was informally explained to the Queen for her implicit approval. The chief officers of the Royal Academy are also among the few British subjects with the privileged right of direct personal access to the Sovereign. They do not often avail themselves of this constitutional freedom, but the President and Secretary of the Royal Academy are normally received in private audience once a year: the Queen invests the President with his gold chain and medal of office and signs a document confirming his election. When Sir Charles Wheeler was first elected the Court Circular announced merely that he was "received and submitted the business of the Institution". This is not as formal as it sounds: in reality the Queen likes to chat a little about the Academy's affairs. Apart from the smallest coterie of officials, the Queen was the first to learn of the Academy's increasing financial difficulties and of the proposed sale of its Leonardo cartoon. Unlike the millions who had hitherto never heard of its existence, she could compare the choice with other Academy treasures of no less beauty and high value: Michelangelo's marble bas-relief of the Madonna, for example, or the D'Oggiono copy of Leonardo's *Last Supper*, painted by one of Leonardo's pupils in his lifetime and still in perfect preservation; a picture somewhat harsh in outline, but probably far closer to the great original than the much-restored mural on the walls of the convent of S. Maria delle Grazia in Milan.

The Queen is also always among the first to know of the Academy's forthcoming winter and Diploma Gallery exhibitions. It was not entirely coincidence that the three exhibitions of 1961 — the Age of Charles II and the Landseer and Lawrence exhibitions — all reflected the Academy's close link with the Crown. When the Waterloo Chamber at Windsor Castle was renovated, the Queen herself offered that the sixteen Lawrence portraits should come to the Academy, and she denuded the walls of the dining-room at Balmoral of several pictures for the commemoration of Sir Edwin Landseer that prudently demonstrated her family sentiment to be not unmerited. (In apostrophizing Victorian art, we are conveniently apt to forget that the young Landseer exhibited in the Academy during the reign of George III.) Moreover, in the first decade of her reign, the Queen lent over 500 pictures and works of art to the Academy for exhibition purposes. As many as 207 drawings were loaned to the Leonardo exhibition, fifty-eight pictures to the display of British Portraits — a pageant of the British physiognomy that the Queen privately visited at least twice, as did Princess Margaret — and no fewer than eighty-six of the Queen's pictures, from Giorgiones and Titians to Canaletto wash drawings, were loaned to the winter exhibition of Italian Art that heralded her own State Visit to Italy.

The above would be impressive patronage from any source, but the Queen's interest is equally underwritten by intimate acquaintance. At Professor Richardson's first audience, for instance, the Queen remarked that she would like to visit the Academy schools. No monarch for many years had trodden the back staircase to the basement or penetrated the gloomy corridor along the length of the schoolrooms. Few visitors to the Academy, strolling through Galleries IV to VIII are aware of the students beneath their feet. But the Queen knows. Rarely had there been such painting of corridors, such polishing of windows and skylights, such sprucing of students. The Academicians, after debating presentations and bouquets, dreamed up a symbolic gesture to grace the occasion. A student copied the bust of George III in white plaster and within its pristine fingers was placed a single red rose to give to the Queen. At least one Academician nonetheless found it equally moving and significant when the young queen, still in her twenties, smilingly tried on Sir Joshua Reynolds's spectacles. The Queen had asked to see her hundred students at work, and the painting, drawing, sculpture and architecture classes were accordingly in full session as she toured the building. So it came about that the students no doubt wore their best pullovers and painted the worst pictures of their lives, and the Queen of England talked to a young art student who was paying his way by working part-time as a chef. Presently a young student presented a portfolio of the students' drawings, and thus it happens that representative work of the Academy students of 1955 shares shelf space in the Royal Library at Windsor with the drawings of Leonardo da Vinci.

The Queen is also Patron of the Royal Academy of Dramatic Art, the Royal Academy of Dancing, and the Royal Academy of Music, embodying very similar duties of overseeing, inspection and interest. She is Patron of the Royal Institute of Painters in Water Colour, of the Royal Institute of British Architects, and the Royal Society of British Sculptors. She is "constitutionally" supposed to take an interest in the Royal College of Music, which received its royal charter in 1883, and indeed she conscientiously attended its students' concerts whenever possible and presented its prizes almost every year until she came to the Throne. She extends her patronage to the Royal Amateur Orchestral Society and to the Royal Scottish Dance Society, and her patronage of the Royal Horticultural Society can be included here for those who rank gardening among the higher arts. All the world knows how assiduously the Queen works at her red dispatch boxes of Government papers but, in addition to this voluminous reading, the Queen finds on her desk the annual reports of every society and group in which she is interested, marked and annotated for her attention.

In much the same way as the founding of the Royal Academy, King George IV in 1820 also issued the first instructions for the Royal Society of Literature, and assigned from his Privy Purse an annual subscription of a thousand guineas to provide pensions for ten Royal Associates. It is sad to record that this pleasant stipend died with the King, while a subsequent grant of £100 a year from Queen Victoria, who could well afford it, was suddenly dropped. Today the Queen accords the Royal Society of Literature her patronage and exercises the right of giving an annual Gold Medal for Poetry. First instituted by King George V in 1933, the Gold Medal was significantly awarded to only three recipients — Laurence Whistler, W. H. Auden, and Michael Thwaites — over eighteen years. Perhaps the war or the parlous plight of poetry were to blame. Since her Accession, however, the Queen has made the award to Andrew Young, Arthur Waley, Ruth Pitter, Edmund Blunden, Siegfried Sassoon, Frances Cornford, John Betjeman, and Christopher Fry. In addition, Her Majesty annually subscribes to the Royal Literary Fund, another of George III's great benefices which every year makes grants to authors of published books of merit, or their widows, who have fallen into straightened circumstances, and in a recent average year spread £7,100 among twenty-two applicants.

The Civil List pensions granted by the Royal Bounty Fund, a sum amounting to some £35,000 a year, are, in fact, administered by the Treasury and the recognition thus accorded to composers, poets and painters in their old age need not involve us in controversy. The funds of the Royal Almonry are primarily administered through ecclesiastical channels but, as one of its officials has commented, it should not be assumed that the arts are excluded.

III

It would be absurd, of course, to expect the Queen to be constantly cognizant of all the affairs of all the bodies operating under her patronage or protection, although the Palace authorities stress that the Queen never undertakes the patronage of any society or organization in which she cannot feel real personal interest. Over a hundred organizations, cultural, scientific, social and of the utmost diversity, operate under royal charters, some asserting their privilege since the reign of Charles I. Half as many again are permitted to use the prefix "Royal" and to use the royal coat-of-arms. In the field of the arts alone the Queen's support is expected to range from the Royal Choral Society to the Royal Society of Portrait Painters, from the affairs of the Royal Philharmonic Orchestra

— and even the Royal Albert Hall — to the cultural interests of the Royal Asiatic Society and an infinite range of Commonwealth interests. As Sir Ivor Jennings has pointed out, the Royal Family tries to encourage and take an active part in those efforts of ordinary people which achieve merit. It is concerned as much with art and literature, learning and sport, as with politics. The demands on the Queen's time are limitless, her time limited. But even the most distant overseas organization under her patronage can place its affairs before her at least once a year. A chart of her regular activities, constantly broken though they must be by tours and overseas visits, shows that her visits to concerts, opera and the ballet average twelve a year. Her formal recorded theatre visits average six a year, but many more are unannounced or charted as unofficial. The Queen's official visits to art galleries and art exhibitions average ten a year, and here, too, many such occasions are unreported. Even the purpose of a prearranged and announced public visit, when thousands gather to see her, may escape observant comment under the "human interest" details of what the Queen is wearing or what she says when meeting an old lady of ninety.

Thus, apart from her Academy visits in London, the Queen endeavours to visit the exhibition of the Royal Society of Portrait Painters every winter, a visit that invariably attracts less attention than her presence at the Derby. Whenever possible, her visit to the Antique Dealers Fair in June is as regular a feature of her calendar as her visit to Goodwood in July. The Queen's almost annual attendance at the Royal Film Performance or some equivalent charity film show is matched by her attention to the always memorable performance of Scottish dancing and songs in the forecourt of Holyroodhouse, a romantic spectacle in the gloaming, whenever she is in residence. When in Scotland, too, Her Majesty likes to visit at least the summer exhibition of the Royal Scottish Academy, her lively interest and local knowledge always demonstrating that this is not a dutiful chore to make amends for her Burlington House favours, but a visit of true enjoyment. One year, the Queen visited the Edinburgh Festival from Balmoral, enjoying a concert at the Usher Hall and a Hamburg State Opera performance of *The Magic Flute*. Another year, the medieval mystery plays at York gained her attention; and at the highest level of national artistic achievement the Queen has watched Shakespeare at the Stratford Memorial Theatre and *The Marriage of Figaro* superbly performed at Glyndebourne.

Only an exceptional revision of schedule prevents the Queen from attending a "Royal Concert" in aid of the Musicians' Benevolent Fund at the Festival Hall once in every three years, although the public attention this gains is infinitesimal compared with the column inches of newsprint accorded the annual Royal Variety Performance. When the Queen is visiting towns and cities throughout Britain her programme is largely devised by her hosts, and it is not her fault if civic authorities wish her to see hospitals and schools rather than art galleries or to honour local industrial achievements at the expense sometimes of local tradition and accomplishment in the fine arts. Municipal pride rarely equals the enterprise of the city of Leeds, which not only indulged the Queen with an opera, and a symphony concert at their centenary music festival, but also invited her to see the modern paintings in the City Art Gallery. At Gloucester, on one occasion, the Queen startled her guides and mentors by the amount of time she was prepared to devote to inspecting the work of purely local — and part-time — artists. The Queen's enjoyment of "small occasions" among "friends and neighbours" has similarly been amply demonstrated at concerts at King's Lynn, and the royal support accorded the Royal Choral Society does not prevent the Queen from finding time to attend a performance of *The Dream of Gerontius* by a local choral society of Windsor and Eton.

The Sovereign is, of course, non-partisan, and the Queen cannot publicly give prolonged support to one institution at the expense of another. On her Accession, for example; she could no longer preside over the Royal Society of Arts; instead she consented to succeed her father as Patron, and the Society's Medal, which for five years had borne her profile head, had to be revised. As Princess Elizabeth, she had the pleasure of reopening the Society's Great Room, which had been restored to its former Adams beauty after the bombing, the paintings of Gainsborough and Reynolds and Barry reinstated on the walls. There, too, she presided over the first meeting of the Festival of Britain and attended the first reception of the Faculty of Royal Designers for Industry, a body set up as one of the new gestures of royal approval of King George VI's reign. As Queen she has herself been awarded the Society's Gold Medal to mark her "personal service to Arts, Manufactures and Commerce at home and abroad", and we have demonstrated that the offering was not undeserved.

We have similarly seen the special relationship of the Royal Academy to the Crown, but, at a different level, it is equally interesting to study the Queen's deft impartiality in the intense rivalry of the three great London art schools. Has the Queen visited the Academy school, but perhaps not the Slade? Nevertheless, Sir William Coldstream, the Slade's Principal, has lunched at Buckingham Palace, and his school, attached as it is to the University of London, can pride itself on the two London University men, Sir Anthony Blunt and Mr. Oliver

Millar, who were at Her Majesty's right hand as Surveyor and Deputy Surveyor of the Queen's Pictures. Does this seem to overlook the claims of the Royal College of Art, which was given its royal title by Queen Victoria nearly seventy years ago and responded in the present reign by creating the Queen's Beasts and completing work inside and outside Westminster Abbey for the Coronation? At this writing, the Queen is nominally neither its Patron nor Protector, although the Duke of Edinburgh ranked as a Senior Fellow, in company with Henry Moore, Sir Kenneth Clark, Sir Gordon Russell and others. (But his title has an ironic ring to suspicious students who note that he was originally welcomed as an Honorary Fellow and appears to have been unobtrusively promoted.) "Dealings with artists require great prudence," the College Principal, Robin Darwin, cautioned the Duke on his installation. Professor Darwin was, however, quoting the advice given by the Prince Consort's Uncle Leopold to Queen Victoria: "They (artists) are acquainted with all classes of society and for that reason are very *dangerous*. They are hardly ever satisfied and when you have too much to do with them you are sure to make enemies" — and Robin Darwin went on to express the hope that times had changed. Beneath the slight chill of official nonpatronage of the Royal College, one, in fact, discovers that the reality and strength of royal support is known in acute detail to staff and students. Touring a pottery works at Stoke, the Queen astonished a young designer by inquiring, "You were Royal College of Art, were you not?" She had, no doubt, been primed beforehand. But an annual R.C.A. report that mentioned the student's name had found its way to her desk; the information had been filed and appeared in an aide memoir at the right time. In any reign the link between an art student and the ruling Sovereign has never been more efficiently organized nor of firmer substance.

As we know, the Queen's special interest in the Royal College of Art dates from the Festival of Britain days, when she enjoyed studying the details of preparation of the South Bank Exhibition and discovered the innumerable links with the Royal College, from Hugh Casson's architectural supervision to the murals, the scenic affects and the skills in layout and craftsmanship achieved by past students and present tutors. The Royal College, too, was in a state of flux and reorientation closely corresponding with the then Princess's sense of useful and important emergence in the post-war world. It had been the youngest of the great art schools, its avowed speciality the art of industrial design. Now it had energetically split into over a dozen specialized schools and departments, embracing painting, sculpture, graphic design, ceramics, silversmithing, print-making, textile design, furniture design, fashion design and stained glass. It was in Festival Year itself that Sir Hugh and Lady Casson founded the School of Interior Design, without realizing they would one day supervise rooms for the Queen at Windsor. With fresh and practical emphasis, the reorganized College was directed towards the same "encouragement of arts, manufactures and commerce" for which the Royal Society of Arts had gained its charter. Conscientiously following up everything she undertakes, the former President of the Royal Society of the Arts, on becoming Queen, seems to have found the Royal College of Art a particularly apt foster-child.

Besides, ever since the Prince Consort pleaded for "mechanical skill to be wed with high art", industrial design has been a "safe" non-controversial cause for royal crusaders. "The highest standards in everything ... a special duty on our craftsmen and manufacturers…" Princess Elizabeth's careful words to the Royal Society of Arts echoed more emphatically in the Duke of Edinburgh's Royal College speech, "It will be a great day when it is considered as important to have something shown in the Design Centre as it is to have a picture hung in the Royal Academy. You're lucky if you own a picture painted by a R.A., but most people have got to live with furniture, domestic objects, cars, shops, pubs and everything else…"

Such words end in a ripple of applause, but the ovation was not the end of duty for the Queen and her husband, who often continued with private action. Thus one finds the Queen and the Duke of Edinburgh visiting St. Michael's Church, Linlithgow, and deciding that it would be an excellent idea to present an engraved offertory plate to commemorate their visit. The Queen's Private Secretary asks Professor Darwin if he could recommend a young silversmith who would be suitable to design and make a silver alms dish. The R.C.A. Principal recommends Philip Popham, one of his tutors in silversmithing, who is accordingly commissioned. With zeal and enthusiasm, Philip Popham prepares alternative designs and submits them, suggesting that they might be better seen in half-scale models made up in silver-plated gilding metal. The suggestion is accepted; the models prepared, with photographs of them enlarged to full size, and Her Majesty asks for one of the designs to be made up without alteration. Nor does this conclude the practical demonstration of forthright patronage, for the circular alms dish, engraved and inscribed, must have a silk-lined oak box, which is thereupon joyfully made by a Mr. Lenthall, a young craftsman in the School of Furniture Design. Three years later, moreover, the Queen commissions Philip Popham to design and make a Chalice and Paten to commemorate a visit to St. Mary's Church, Rotterdam.

Patronage of this order resembles a coral strand, that still keeps the greater part of its strength concealed below the surface. To illustrate further, the Duke of Edinburgh endured teatime ceremonial with spirit-lamp and silver tea-kettle for a time and then sent the ornate Victorian kettle to the College for students to exercise their skill in electrification. The Queen decided that her bathroom must have new curtains; the work of five students of textile design is submitted and the Queen chose a rose design by Brenda Noble which was duly printed and put into use. Or again the Queen Mother was presented with an illuminated document and a commission given for it be designed and printed by students of the R.C.A. school of graphic design. With all this, it seems fitting that the hooped yew cot used by Prince Andrew should have been designed by Mr. Frank Guille of the College's school of furniture design, the rails embossed with silver and enamel escutcheons of nursery animals designed by silversmithing students.

To those interested in tracing all the chain-link fencing of the Establishment, it might be misleading to mention that Colonel Robert Adeane, cousin of the Queen's Private Secretary, was prominent on the College council. More to the point, the Royal College has also had its fair representation at the famous Palace luncheons. The Principal, Professor Robin Darwin; the head of the Faculty of Graphic Design, Sir Hugh Casson; his opposite number in the Faculty of Fine Arts, Professor Carel Weight; Council members such as Sir Frederick Hooper, Sir Gordon Russell and Osbert Lancaster have all been "among those present". In equal line of royal duty, the College has had visits from the Queen Mother and Princess Alexandra. From time to time, the Queen certainly sees *Ark*, the rebellious, witty magazine produced by R.C.A. students, with its vivid styling, constant experiment in technique, youthful intensity and panache. She thus keeps in touch with the new movements of the youthful art world, with each fresh viewpoint on the function of the artist. Indeed, in attention to the Anti-Ugly Association, which started within the College, the Queen instructed that no television aerials should disfigure Windsor Castle. She has similarly shown a direct and questioning interest in the new and modernist Royal College buildings, which are fittingly next door to her great-great-grandmother's pet artistic panjandrum, the Albert Hall. Lunching with the Queen, or in conversation during portraiture sessions, artists find her well acquainted with contemporary movements. If we assume that the Queen has sometimes "done her homework" for these occasions, this affords a measure of constant effort that is far from indifference. When the Queen attended the consecration of Coventry Cathedral she could reflect that she had watched this distinguished artistic and architectural landmark of our era from its inception. She had taken pleasure in John Piper's smallest Windsor drawings, and now he had designed the great Baptistery window; she had commissioned paintings from Graham Sutherland and now could see the finished achievement of his High Altar tapestry; there was much else and no doubt, above all, she could admire the Royal College of Art's special contribution, the stained-glass windows of the nave, with a sense of friendship and participation.

6: NEW WINDS AND CROSS-CURRENTS

Buckingham Palace faces west to the gardens and east to the Mall, as perhaps all the world knows, and in the past twenty years the Ambassadors' Entrance on the southern side, faulted for its proximity to the kitchen entrance, has declined in customary usage. Ambassadors presenting their Letters of Credence are nowadays nobly received at the Grand Entrance within the eastern courtyard, but, for garden parties and more splendid occasions, diplomats, ministers and others with the right of Entrée still continue to use the broad southern corridor. It remains the passageway of the privileged.

Until recently little else enhanced its lustre. The sun-ray clock within the vestibule indeed reminded King George V of a cinema. Apart from a portrait gallery of stern old admirals, the walls were obliterated by the series of large, dark and rather dull canvases which the Van de Veldes, as "Painters of Sea Fights to Their Majesties", at a remuneration of £100 a year, had covered with smoky episodes of naval warfare and piracy. For the rest, forty yards of the corridor was hung with a panorama of the Coronation procession of William IV painted by R. B. Davis, an extraordinary work in five lengths with hundreds of figures and horses, admirably drawn and richly coloured, but none the less dated and daunting. Today it has been replaced by the vigorous, exhilarating, 62-feet-long panel of the Queen's Coronation procession by Feliks Topolski, idiosyncratic, exotic with modern colouring, briskly challenging any visitors who may share the illusion that the traditional continuity of the monarchy is ossified and unchanging and survives only from the past.

Between the windows, opposite the large main panel, hang six smaller panels of the Abbey ceremony, filled equally with Topolski's spidery and impetuous grotesqueries, their Cruickshank irreverence far removed from flattery. It was the Duke of Edinburgh, we know, who commissioned these panels, yet Topolski brings visitors face to face with a new and disturbing vision of the Queen, in her own house and by her consent. The pasteboard impression of dutiful discipline and formality fades a little. This is the Queen Elizabeth II who has the Order of Merit as the highest distinction in her personal bestowal, apart from the ancient orders of knighthood, and embellishes her reign by conferring it upon Graham Sutherland and Sir Basil Spence. This is the Queen who invites Henry Moore, Benjamin Britten, and John Piper to lunch — and Giles, too, for fair measure — or rather shyly discusses literature over the table with Cicely Wedgwood and Freya Stark.

One points the contrast with Queen Victoria, who kept Dickens standing in conversation for an hour and a half when he was lame and sick, three months before his death, and then presented him with a copy of her *Journal of Our Life in the Highlands* and asked in return for a set of his works, to be sent in if possible that same afternoon. Queen Victoria did not murder Charles Dickens, and her Counsel for the Defence may plead that the Queen also stood all the time herself. But compare this again with Elizabeth II, who, amid the modern glories of Coventry Cathedral, did not forget to comment, "How nice the hassocks are!" because she knew that a group of volunteers had worked on the embroidered kneelers as a labour of love. Queen Victoria was impregnable. Her great-

great-granddaughter, Queen Elizabeth, looked rather sadly at specimens of a Crown Derby dinner service proposal for presentation to her, and commented, "I don't always want to be gazing at my own cypher." (Subsequently the manufacturers received a note tactfully intimating that if the cypher had to be used at all, it should be on the back.)

Another illuminating indication of character can be drawn from Windsor. When the Royal Borough decided not long ago to co-operate with the Civic Trust in a planning scheme to improve the amenities of the town, removing ugly shop advertisements and street signs, co-ordinating the colour schemes of rival property-owners and so forth, the Corporation did not seek or find any cause for participation from the Castle. But the Queen had no sooner heard of the Windsor Project than she suggested that the Castle itself might be scrutinized. Later she approved the removal of a six-foot Victorian outer wall, leaving grass banks running unimpeded to the pavement. Yet this was not done without the Queen expressing some disapproval of the shade of pink paint used for a town building then brought into sharper juxtaposition with the approach view to the Castle.

Architects aside, it is usually forgotten that the Queen annually awards an international gold medal for architectural achievement. Acting on the advice of the Royal Institute of British Architects, she would probably not dream of deferring a recommendation. But she has shown in discussion that she studies the work of those commended to her with a lively eye and is by no means a passive donor. The gold medal has been called "the greatest compliment architects can pay any architect" and in the present reign it has so far been awarded to Grey Wornum and John Easton of Great Britain, Gropius, Mies van der Rohe and Lewis Mumford of the U.S.A., Le

Corbusier of France, Sir A. G. Stephenson of Australia, Schofield Morris of Canada, Alvar Aalto of Finland, Luigi Nervi of Italy and, in 1962, Sven Markelius of Sweden.

In quite another field, one might mention that the Queen authorized the Goldsmiths' Company to hold a competition for designs for three Ascot race cups. No limit was set to the submissions, except that designs were to be original yet pay due regard to tradition and include the Royal Arms. In the event, a young Kentish art student, Mr. R. A. Bray, won the £100 first prize for an Ascot Gold Cup to be made in 9-carat gold and Mr. E. M. Dinkel's design was selected for the Royal Hunt Cup in silver-gilt. The open competition was not an innovation, for it had been inaugurated by King George V in 1926 and revived by King George VI in 1939, 1940, 1946 and 1947. But the contest is now an annual one, and the incentive to young British craftsmen is considerable, for between two and three hundred designs are submitted every year. There remain many other royally sponsored contests for racing, yachting and other sporting trophies and medals that deserve to be better known. The Duke of Edinburgh's Trophy for marksmanship, for instance, entailed the commission of a gold-and-silver drinking cup by Maurice Lambert, R.A. Even the design of the medals given to schoolchildren to commemorate an overseas tour may entail patronage. The royal visit to Nigeria in 1956 involved the manufacture of over a million pin-on medals and took up Birmingham's entire output of safety pins for several weeks.

It is unavoidable that modern royal patronage more frequently favours the silversmith or the worker in metal than the sculptor in stone. It was an imaginative gesture when the Queen commissioned Oscar Nemon to execute a bust of Sir Winston Churchill to stand beside the bust of his ancestor, the

Duke of Marlborough, in the Guard Chamber at Windsor Castle, but such opportunities are uncommon. The Queen's Beasts, made for Coronation year, stood ranged in St. George's Hall for a time and had to be removed, so dire was the effect of overcrowding. On the other hand, the Queen seldom misses a visit to the summer exhibition of the Royal Academy and often buys pictures, though intimating that this should not be made known. The jealousies or dismay that might otherwise arise round the royal choice need no emphasis. "There are oddities in there this year, Mr. President," the Queen remarked in 1956, though whether she had in mind the street scenes by Carel Weight, the offerings by Lowry or the fugitive abstracts, was never clear. The President at all events assured her there would be "worse next year". The Queen likes to give pictures to her friends and significantly the only indirect hint of these unpublicized, unhurried visits to the Academy was in 1958, when Prince Philip officially visited the summer show alone because the Queen was ill.

II

One is tempted again into some examination of the crosscurrents and interplay of artistic taste between the Queen and the Duke of Edinburgh as husband and wife. The Duke has made many speeches on the right use of leisure and many on the rightful prestige of good design, and if he appeared to some to overstress the value of physical recreation, we may also remember that the arts syllabi of the Duke of Edinburgh's Award embraces over a score of subjects ranging from painting "any imagined scene" to writing a poem or a one-act play. Public attention is apt to focus on the adventurous overland treks and mountain climbs, but the gold medals and gilt brooches are awarded for a sketchbook of architectural drawings, an essay in literary biography or a piece of creative choreography for amateur ballet, among other qualifications. The Duke was still in his twenties when he approached the brothers Vincent and William Apap in Malta, and commissioned the eight satiric and witty coloured caricature statuettes of British public figures, including Sir Winston Churchill and Earl Mountbatten, which he kept arrayed on a shelf in his Sandringham study. The Queen with graver insight saw the possibilities of an Apap portrait bust of Prince Philip, and the royal couple later commissioned from Vincent Apap a bust of the Prince of Wales and from his brother a half-length portrait of Princess Anne. To be precise, both were commissioned by Prince Philip. But we can distinguish the interplay of two minds in strengthening maturity, and who can separate the decisions of executive consort or prompting spouse, or time the pace of improving discrimination?

Prince Philip attended the crowded preview of the 1960 Picasso exhibition at the Tate and was thought careless because he left the congested gallery after some forty minutes of presentations had been completed against the background of intense and disdainful paint. Yet he returned with the Queen another evening, after the public had left, to spend two-and-a-half hours in undisturbed attention to the sumptuous pageant of Picasso's works. The Queen can rarely visit a gallery and lose herself in rapt contemplation of a picture. Visits of even the most private and informal nature see the attentive host or the diligent guide at her elbow. One cannot fathom the emotional *rapport* offered by one painter or another, but it can be deduced that the Queen's sympathies are more assured, her range of comparison and her powers of analysis wider than is commonly thought.

The Queen Mother, Patron of the Contemporary Art Society and of the Friends of the Tate Gallery, had herself nurtured and heightened her daughter's sensibilities, as we have seen. (In passing, the Queen Mother was also Patron of the Royal Society of Painters in Water-Colours, the Royal Scottish Society of Arts and the Royal Cambrian Academy of Art, among others.) Princess Margaret was also extremely interested in modern art and had two small paintings by Anthony Fry, a John Piper, a piece by Jean de Maol and other contemporary paintings in a necessarily small but eclectic collection. With her husband, Lord Snowdon, she followed current artistic event as diverse as the London murals of William Mitchell, the latest fireworks of Soulages or the findings of the international juries, seeking to satisfy herself, however, rather than merely sustain artistic conversation.

One might join issue then with Mr. Kingsley Martin's contention in his book *The Crown and the Establishment* that the Royal Family has not been interested in contemporary artistic development since the death of George IV. Perhaps it would have been better if the "unofficial" Queen's Royal Academy acquisitions had been publicized, now that John Bratby, Anne Redpath, A. S. Lowry, James Fitton, John Skeaping and Edward Bawden are authoritatively within its confines. Yet we may consider again the Queen's announced contemporary purchases: Graham Sutherland, Alan Davie, Barbara Hepworth, Sidney Nolan, Mary Fedden, Roger de Grey, Robin Darwin, Denis Wirth-Miller, Ivon Hitchens — characterized in 1962 as one of the most representative English painters of our day — James Taylor, Kenneth Rowntree, Anna Zinkeisen, John Piper, Edward Seago, Peter Scott and so many others. If it is true that the ideal collector buys only pictures with something to convey personally, sustains a strong sympathy for the artist, and buys only with integrity unaffected by fads of name or fashion, the Queen clearly qualifies. The favourite better-known pictures of Queen Elizabeth the Queen Mother admittedly bear an older flavour, her Sickerts and Johns and Sisleys, her cool Wilson Steer, her pictures by Matthew Smith, Duncan Grant and William Nicholson, even her *Landscape of the Vernal Equinox* by Paul Nash, but the reputations of these artists remain iridescent among the creative talent of her time.

In 1962, one of the Queen Mother's continuing but unpublicized purchases happened to be divulged when she acquired two dockland scenes by Rodney Johnson. Here was a young art teacher who had scarcely dreamed of a private exhibition of his paintings, let alone royal patronage. The Queen Mother chanced to see one of his pictures in a private home, admired the style of dusky, scenic impressionism veering towards the abstract, and later bought two out of three of his pictures submitted to her. In the same way, the Queen once happened to see one of the popular reproductions of the late Christopher Wood's firm little seascape, *The Red Funnel*, and, admiring the strongly painted tugs against the rough blue-green sea, Her Majesty subsequently acquired the original from Mrs. Lucy Wertheim. This best-selling print had been judged an excellent picture for a boy's room and perhaps the Queen was deftly guiding the taste of the Prince of Wales.

The Queen Mother patronized the young John Piper, after he had already passed through his abstract phase and was ripe for his notable topographical studies of Windsor. The Duke of Edinburgh, meanwhile, commissioned twenty-four Windsor drawings from Alan Carr Linford, one of the youngest members of the Royal Society of Watercolourists. Of these, twelve show precisely the same views that Sandby painted in the days of George III, and for the rest Mr. Linford's choice of scene was his own. Royal facilities of an exceptional nature were also accorded to Mr. Edward Seago when he joined Prince Philip aboard the royal yacht *Britannia* for the 1956–7 world tour and returned with over sixty paintings — ranging from the Antarctic to Gibraltar — which were subsequently exhibited for charity at St. James Palace. The Queen looked indulgently on her husband's enthusiasms. Having bought Seago's *Portrait of a Grey Horse* in 1956, she visited his 1960 exhibition at Colnaghi's, as if blending a collector's instinct with friendly interest in the work of a Norfolk neighbour.

The Duke of Edinburgh painted and practised a little lino-cutting under Seago's eye and he has continued to paint as a hobby, a relaxation he had in common with President Kennedy. In a book on Prince Philip's leisure, this author mentions that he sought Annigoni's advice on the techniques of paint preparation and glazing and presently produced some of his own landscapes of Windsor and Balmoral for a critical opinion. Approving a remarkable colour sense and fine perspective, the master detected brave brush strokes denoting a grasp and force unusual in a beginner. But Annigoni knew little of the hours of quiet application in the painting-room at Gordonstoun where the individual "Project of skill, intellectual or practical" calls for a boy to complete a painting, a piece of sculpture or an architectural model, as an essay in self-reliant endeavour. With the school orchestra, the literary society and the pottery class, these are opportunities as readily available to the heir to the Throne as they were to his father — though less publicized than the overwritten exploits of the coastguard patrol or the school fire brigade — and in his first term at Gordonstoun Prince Charles already produced some pleasant examples of pottery.

Speaking at the Design Centre, Prince Philip once said he had no personal experience of design, but this disclaimer was modest. He sketched the intricate pattern for a richly worked compact which Stephen Gooden, R.A., completed in platinum for presentation to the Queen, and he had tried his hand at several such ventures. After a Victorian tea-kettle had been successfully electrified for the Duke at the Royal College of Arts, he supplied the detailed and illustrated specifications for a tea-kettle on a bracket stand with ivory mounts, incorporating several improvements on standard types, which tutors and students then made up. We need scarcely mention the Duke of Edinburgh's Prize for Elegant Design, which has been awarded for a refrigerator, a transistor radio, a tea service and a range of furnishing fabrics. Less familiar is the trophy of a dog collar in solid silver which he personally designed for the Prince Philip Stakes, a greyhound racing event held in aid of the Duke of Edinburgh's Award Scheme.

If Prince Philip's practical eye sometimes tempts him to take too ludicrous a view of abstract art, this is no more than the closest humour required at times from all but the most asseverant disciples. "My goodness, they're asking £900 for it!" he once exclaimed at an unusually esoteric expression of Scottish sculpture; and a blue-spiked pattern by the Chilean artist, Guillermo Nunes, caused him to inquire, "Who perpetrated this?" In youthful company, the bubbling impulse of a royal quip proved irresistible, as when he presented a Henry Moore bronze as the Prince Philip Prize for zoology pupils and remarked, "It looks like a monkey's gallstone." Headlines froze the jest next day. Many of the paintings the Duke has bought for Holyroodhouse can be ranked in turn as accomplished but unconventional. One turns to precedents. The Prince Consort, assiduous with drawing-board and easel, was capable of telling Frith how he might better *Derby Day*. "He told me why I had done certain things," wrote Frith, "and how, if a certain change had been made, my object would have been assisted. How the masses of light and shade might be still more evenly balanced, and how some parts of the picture might receive still more completion..." The Duke of Edinburgh, forthright though he was, could never be guilty of such rash, royal egoism.

III

The Queen does not paint. It was enough to have Queen Victoria sending her watercolours to all the crowned heads of Europe, an accumulation of mementos now liable to impose on her descendants an exacting struggle between respect and derision. What the old Queen did not attempt was duly achieved by her daughter, Princess Louise, who intrepidly exhibited sculpture at the Royal Academy and sculpted the imposing monument to her mother outside Kensington Palace, as well as filling Windsor Castle with watercolours. The Duke of Edinburgh had been known to consign his own paintings, still lifes and landscapes alike, to the incinerators or to wield his scissors on a string of sketches on cartridge paper for re-use in an architectural model. Princess Marina, the Duchess of Kent, though occasionally cajoled into placing a charcoal and pastel drawing on exhibition for charity, never devoted much wall-space to her own efforts. The Queen's drawing lessons as a young girl produced work described as painstaking and thorough, but she never shared Princess Margaret's deft sketching ability. More often the Queen's chief means of artistic expression is her film camera, and leisure at Windsor and Sandringham is often devoted to producing and editing her own travelogues and family movies.

theThat the Queen has a trained and percipient eye is undisputed. At Gloucester, on being shown some signed documents of Elizabeth I's reign and asked if she could distinguish the Queen's original signature from those clerically forged by her courtiers, she quickly and accurately sifted the autographs. A Barlaston pottery triumphantly preserves a black basalt bowl on which the Queen tried her hand with a leaf pattern with fair effect. Although Annigoni has latterly fallen out of favour with the critics, the part that the Queen herself played in "discovering" him in England may be remembered. Visiting an exhibition at the Royal Society of Portrait Painters, Her Majesty paused for a long time to admire the portrait of Mrs. Christie Miller, which the then comparatively unknown artist had sent from Florence.

"Who painted that?" she asked Mr. James Gunn, who was showing her round. "I think it's beautiful. I hope one day he will be able to paint me."

Such a hint is a command, and none was better pleased than the Queen when the attraction of the Annigoni portrait drew more than a quarter-million people to "her" Royal Academy and eclipsed all attendance records for forty years. In the huge and dissembling arena of portraiture, the Queen's interest in such artists as Terence Cuneo, Anthony Devas and many others fully demonstrates her maturing capacity to distinguish between the original and the pastiche. It is informing to chart some of the Queen's visits to the art shows, from the obvious interest in iconography and event of the Terence Cuneo exhibition in 1954, and Her Majesty's leisurely inspection of the notable Monets, Van Goghs, and Cezannes during a private visit to the Courtauld Institute gallery five years later. The Queen inspected the show of equestrian pictures at Leggatt's Galleries in the winter of 1959 and again went to the similar display at the Frank Partridge rooms the following year, but on both occasions Christmas gifts were in the air and both exhibitions were held under charitable auspices. The Queen has occasionally seen Academy exhibitions when they were still in preparation, with pictures unhung or disarranged. Equally, the broad variety of her interests is demonstrated by her private visit to an exhibition of Steuben glass and a Scottish visit to a commemorative display of the works of Raeburn.

An occasion more out of the common run occurred in 1957, when the Weinburg collection of moderns was sent from America for auction at Sotheby's and the Queen specially visited the salerooms one evening for a private view. She inspected paintings by Cezanne, Renoir, Boudin, Fantin-Latour, Signac, Buffet and others, but in reality her interest was far more personal, focused as it was on Monet's fine *Blue House at Zaandam*. Queen Elizabeth the Queen Mother had purchased Monet's *The Rock* from Wildenstein's in 1945; to this the *Blue House* formed a perfect companion piece, and it is evident that the Queen hoped to acquire it as a gift for her mother's birthday four weeks ahead.

Unluckily, the intended surprise was to end in disappointment, for the saleroom ignores loyalties and knows only one standard: the highest bid. Four months later, while looking at a Monet group in the National Gallery of Art in Washington, the Queen confessed to John Walker, the Gallery director, that she had been thinking of Monet. She had indeed, she said, set her heart on acquiring the *Blue House*, but that the bidding went to a staggering figure. The picture, in fact, made £22,000.

Nearly a year later the Queen similarly honoured the premises of Christie's, when she visited their rooms to view the treasures of the Chatsworth collection. Not that this was intended as a demonstration of impartial royal favour to the two great firms of art auctioneering. As it happened, the Queen was highly interested in a Gainsborough portrait which had been sent in for sale by Lord Waldegrave just at that time. This was a full-length painting of William Henry, Duke of Gloucester, one of the few Gainsborough portraits of an adult member of George III's family not to be found in the Crown collection. As a picture, however, it can be regarded as one of Gainsborough's failures. Indeed, even the artist left it unfinished, and the Queen's enthusiasm was not maintained. Her Majesty was more interested in a picture by Giovanni Pellegrini, a decorative rococo painter who collected for Consul Smith and whom the Queen thinks ripe for greater appreciation than he has hitherto enjoyed. The Queen also studied the pictures by Van Dyck and Schiavone, the notable pieces of Chatsworth silver, the silver-gilt toilet set of the age of Louis XVI, the twenty-four dinner plates bearing the cypher of William III which had undoubtedly become a perquisite of his Lord Steward of the Household. But she made no purchases. In the event, the Waldegrave picture was acquired by Leggatt Brothers with a bid of twenty-one thousand guineas on behalf of a client who wished to remain anonymous, and although Leggatt's held an exclusive warrant of Appointment to Queen Elizabeth the Queen Mother, I have been authoritatively assured that no member of the Royal Family was the buyer.

The Queen's Monet loss was in any event a fluke, for pictures by him have since been sold for £16,000, £19,500 and as high as £105,000. Like most of us, the Queen has no real idea of saleroom values. She regularly receives and studies catalogues from Christie's and Sotheby's, but they are marked for her attention solely for the intrinsic interest of the pictures, furniture or *objets d'art* coming on to the market and not in any sense for investment. In watching the catalogues, the Queen still pursues Queen Mary's treasure-hunt for pieces known to be missing, leading lost royal sheep back to the fold. Royal interest in a coming sale item is rarely made known, and the Queen's agents frequently allow themselves to be outbid. But this factor, coupled with anonymity, in itself frequently achieves negotiations at reasonable levels. Thus the Queen acquired fifty-two volumes of the manuscript notebooks and diaries of Joseph Farington at Christie's for only £165, on a day when everyone else must have been dozing. When Agnew's handled six views of Windsor by Paul Sandby, royal interest seemed assured, and they were, in fact, acquired for the Queen for only £408, a clear bargain compared with the £860 asked at the same gallery in 1962 for two of Sandby's watercolours of Welsh castles.

Royal purchases are seldom publicized and the skilful devolution of royal duties also creates a useful smokescreen of royal intentions beforehand. Mr. Oliver Millar, as Deputy Surveyor of the Queen's Pictures, or Mr. Mackworth-Young, custodian of the royal library at Windsor, may be separately concerned, but they showed habitual interest in too many items for their real interest in any one to be identified. Their extremely close attention to the market was typified when a portrait of Charles I, said to be by Jacob van Doordt, was offered at the country house sale at Cobham Hall in 1957. In reality, it was a portrait by Mytens, who had painted all the finer and more elegant portrayals of the King before the arrival of Van Dyck. The Queen acquired it for only £240 and under its true attribution it has now joined the gallery of State portraits at St. James's Palace. Miss Scott-Elliot similarly displayed true knowledge and acumen when she purchased without hesitation a miniature of Hugh May by Samuel Cooper which came privately on the market in 1958. This was a rare prize, for May, as Controller of Works at Windsor, had been in charge of the extensive rebuilding under Charles II. Royal transactions such as these are occurring almost continuously. The Queen similarly bought a family portrait by Jacopo Amigoni and it was announced in 1962 that she had purchased one of Graham Sutherland's sketches for the Coventry tapestry.

Acquisitions in this field equally fall from time to time within the "special mission" of Lord Plunket, officially Deputy Master of the Queen's Household, but unofficially one of the Queen's special informants in matters of art. Himself the possessor of a prized Rubens and other pictures, it had become his provenance to keep the Queen in touch with artistic news. The Queen regularly sees such magazines as *The Burlington*, *The Connoisseur* and *Apollo*, but there are wider topics she may overlook. If a gallery should show a picture which the Queen might wish to see, it usually devolved on Lord Plunket to arrange a viewing at Buckingham Palace. He appears, for instance, to have been an intermediary in the affair of Hogarth's *George II, Queen Caroline and Their Seven Children*. This was another prize in niche-filling, a painting commissioned by George III, but repudiated by the King because he felt the artist had depicted his Foot Guards in a contemptuous and satiric fight in another picture, and lost to the Crown collection ever since. It appeared at the Antique Dealers Fair priced at £2,500, and nothing more was heard of it, least of all that it had been purchased by the Queen, until Her Majesty lent it to the exhibition of "English Taste in the Eighteenth Century" at the Royal Academy Exhibition some months later.

It denotes no grudging inattentiveness to contemporary art if the Queen maintains particular interest in the completeness and unity of her great classical heritage and takes special pride in the quality, accuracy of attribution, unimpeachable maintenance and perfection of display of the royal pictures and works of art. Any interest the Queen may have in the modern achievements of, say, the Venice Biennale leans not unnaturally to the British triumphs. In conversation her knowledge of the newest contemporary vogue has been called "well above average", but she is not ashamed to say of the work of an unfamiliar artist, "I don't think I know him". She has no reason to be well versed in Giacometti or the abstractions of Manessier, and her closest acquaintance with surrealism is perhaps in the Salvador Dali drawings that adorn the guest suite at Broadlands. (But these were endearingly familiar after many weekend visits to the Mountbatten home.) Especially in earlier years, the Queen was susceptible to the influence of her closest friends, and special recognition must be paid to the late Countess Mountbatten in this sense. Lady Mountbatten was always *au fait* with the latest painters who had won attention (though she seldom patronized them), the newest best-sellers (though she was inclined only to browse in the score or more stacked on her tables), and the latest plays and films (though she had too little time for the theatre). She had the gift of conveying her enthusiasms, whether for Levy's book *Painting for All* or Wheatcroft's *My Life With Roses*, Anna Zinkeisen's pictures or T. S. Eliot's poems, for Freya Stark or Dylan Thomas. Like the Queen, she had come into a great classical heritage of pictures by Van Dyck, Rubens, Lely, Opie, Veronese, Tintoretto, and Canaletto. In the drawing-room at Broadlands the paintings by Romney and Hoppner, Reynolds and Lawrence, echo Windsor Castle itself. We have seen how the Queen in girlhood compared the ceiling paintings by Cipriani at Broadlands with the paintings by the same artist on the Coronation coach. The similar paintings by Angelica Kauffmann, the Guardis and an extraordinary picture in the Broadlands dining-room, originally a flower painting by Jean Baptiste, but painted over both by Reynolds, who added an abstract "eye of friendship", and finally by Lawrence, who achieved a complete portrait of Lady Hamilton as a Bacchante — all these have also held the Queen's interest. Dining with Earl Mountbatten of Burma in Wilton Crescent, the Queen and Prince Philip similarly dine under the smiling gaze of a Frans Hals Dutchwoman and a Reynolds lady: the house can indeed claim Reynolds, Raeburn or Romney in every main room.

The atmosphere is not markedly different when the Queen goes to Goodwood or Badminton or stays with the Wernhers at Luton Hoo. At Goodwood again there are Van Dycks of Charles I and his family, Canalettos, Romneys and Raeburns. If the Duke of Richmond and Gordon is the foremost enthusiast of Goodwood motor-racing, he is also an ardent flower painter, finding his own way by laying the paint on thick with a palette knife. A complete book might be written to demonstrate that a cultivated interest in the arts and an energetic devotion to sport are not a destructive schism, but two mutual, massive bulwarks of the characteristically English way of life. At Badminton also there are Canalettos and portraits by Reynolds, Lawrence, Lely, and Kneller, claiming attention as well as the horse trials. Luton Hoo has a museum room completely dedicated to the Turf relics of Brown Jack but the private rooms of the house are no less replete in Reynolds and Van Dyck, Beechey and Angelica Kauffmann. But we may ring the changes a little, for the dining-room has one of Goya's passionate full-length paintings of the Duchess of Alba, and Luton Hoo shares with Buckingham Palace pride in possessing some of the superb pieces of French furniture stamped by Oeben. Tracing the fusion of sport and art is indeed fascinating. Even the Queen Mother's devotion to steeplechasing was matched by the shared artistic enthusiasms evident in the Renoirs, Boudins, portraits by Augustus John and heads by Epstein to be seen at Fairlawne, the home of Peter Cazalet, her racing trainer.

The pattern has promise, but may lead into error. To trace influences is imperative, and yet the Queen's taste — and especially her interest in twentieth-century achievement — is firmly based on her sense of history of art and the immemorial background of taste and design. It was highly characteristic that, when visiting the Academy exhibition of "The Age of Charles II" a walnut chair excited her eager interest: she asked for it to be turned upside down so that she might see, not the royal brand mark of a C.R. surmounted by a crown but the far rarer initials "W.P." for Whitehall Palace. In her own milieu, the Queen learned with interest and pleasure of the discovery during a cleaning process of the signature of Giachetti on a Louis XVI cabinet in Buckingham Palace. The signature, that of a celebrated employee of the Gobelins factory, is a notable rarity, and Her Majesty was as pleased as you or I might be if we discovered a Roman coin in the garden. To cap this, three black and gold corner cupboards were placed on view in the Queen's Gallery only shortly after the stamp BVRB had been proved to be the initials of Bernard van Risamburgh. He was a French *maître* before 1735–65 and today the very street where he practised his craft in Paris has been identified.

Similarly, when Marlborough House was undergoing renovation for its new use as a Commonwealth Centre, the

Queen was informed of the discovery of vast areas of overpainting on the staircase murals and she hurried round at once to see what was happening. Shortly after the building of Marlborough House, the French artist, Louis Laguerre, had executed a series of large murals on both the main west and the smaller east staircases, showing incidents and central scenes in the Duke of Marlborough's battles. During the widowhood of Queen Adelaide they were papered over as being too dilapidated to repair. After the house was settled on the Prince of Wales, the future Edward VII, they were uncovered and partly restored, but then overpainted to soften their ruthless and unpalatable battle realism. Years of varnishing and overpainting in this way had totally obscured their true nature until the present reign, when the Queen was among the first to encourage the restorers and they scraped away twenty layers of dark overpaint to reveal the bright original, a remarkable contemporary record of soldiery in their seventeenth-century uniforms. It was a notable achievement for Ministry of Works craftsmen and a special satisfaction to the Queen, who paid several visits to watch work in progress.

The days are past when anyone could emulate the Prince Consort and find, as he did, a cache of forgotten pictures in the cellars of Hampton Court, but the perennial quest still has its prospects. The present reign has been notable for the new scrutiny of royal pictures by X-ray, ultra-violet and other probing instruments. The Crown collection has long had a picture under Titian's name entitled *Titian and a Friend*. Reading left to right it might equally well have been called, *Titian, a Friend and Shadow* for a dark space lay to the left of the central figure. The X-ray revealed a third face which cleaning has brought into clear definition. But is it the work of Titian? In such dilemmas the scholarship of Sir Anthony Blunt comes into its own. The friend is now identified as Andrea dei Franceschi and was probably painted by Titian. The two companions have been relegated to the brushes of pupils. But beneath all there lies an unfinished three-quarter length portrait of a fourth man, and another face heightening the theory of a piece of scrap canvas used in Titian's studio school. Meticulous examination of this order brings loss as well as gain. The Queen's Rembrandts and Rubens, her Tintorettos and Correggios, emerged unscathed from the ordeal of investigation. Prince Albert has been upheld and proved to be not deceived in his Cranachs and Fra Angelicos. The early Holbeins had to yield ground as early imitations. On the other hand, the Queen's watchful interest was richly rewarded when the Windsor portrait of Sir Henry Guildford, open to question on whether it was a true Holbein, recently underwent modern cleaning and yielded an undisputable Holbein signature. A much-disputed Rembrandt portrait of a lady similarly was proved under X-ray to have been painted by one, Drost, though it may be a copy of a lost original. The portrait of *David Garrick and his Wife* by Hogarth puzzled the connoisseur by the plainness of its grey-green background, but the penetrating X-ray has disclosed bookshelves, a mirror, candle-sconces and the attributes of a lively background far more Hogarthian in atmosphere. More important still, the Rubens pictures of *Summer* and *Winter* at Buckingham Palace were thought to be companion pieces, but X-rays have shown them to be of different age. Again, a Mytens portrait of Charles I and his Queen long hung high over a door of the Blue Drawing Room in Buckingham Palace, unconsidered and almost too high for serious study. The X-rays reveal changes in the figure of the Queen undertaken by a later hand and the trend of evidence indeed is that the picture was corrected by Van Dyck.

This process of authentication still goes on. Pictures which hitherto hung in dark and lofty corners at Hampton Court have been cleaned, revealing unsuspected refinements. The Queen's Canalettos are being dated by an assiduous process of close examination and comparison. In an art world constantly in pursuit of names and changing values the complete integrity and scholarship surrounding the Queen's pictures is one of the anchorages of stability.

7: THE DIPLOMACY OF ART

I

The link between the cultural and artistic inclinations of a ruler and the prestige of a Court has long received the scrutiny of historians. The theme can be traced from the Medicis of Florence to the Versailles of the Sun King and far beyond, but nowadays the emollient efficacy of art in diplomatic affairs is seldom noticed, save by the diplomats and by the Queen herself. We have studied the Queen in her ambience of celebrated art, yet evidence is not lacking that, apart from "the refreshment of the spirit and the food of thought", the Queen recognizes art as one of the paramount forces of human kinship and employs it with adept skill and intelligence as one of the potent tools of her craft. The night before attending a farewell dinner to Mr. John Hay Whitney on his retirement as American Ambassador, for example, the Queen took the trouble to visit the Tate Gallery, where his collection of pictures was then on view. Less diligent guests might have been content to share Zoffany and Romney as a common enthusiasm. For the Queen it was not enough to study a catalogue and recall the Corots and Cezannes she had already seen on the walls of Winfield House; she evidently wished to be conversant with the paintings by Derain and Fauve, as well as the Van Goghs and Picassos, and no doubt desired to acquaint herself with the work of Wyeth and Fosburgh, modern American paintings which, though unfashionable, had also been bought by Mr. Whitney with enthusiasm. The Tate also offered the personal appeal of the Géricault horse, considered by some the most horse-like horse ever in paint, and *The False Start* by Degas, the first of his studies of the racetrack, but the Queen primarily went out of her way to please her host.

Next, on receiving Mr. David Bruce as the succeeding American Ambassador to the Court of St. James's, a common interest was immediately and smoothly established by his work as a trustee of the National Gallery of Art. Over three years had passed since the Queen had toured the gallery in Washington, where she had particularly admired Rembrandt's *The Mill*, a Donatello *Madonna and Child*, Constable's *Wivenhoe Park*, and a modern American al fresco portrait *The Skater* by Gilbert Stuart. These were but four notables in a vast collection, but Her Majesty had also tried out an electronic guide system, using a transistor radio and earpiece to tour the room of El Grecos, and remembered the experience with evident pleasure. (The Queen has, in fact, since given permission for excerpts from her own speeches to be used on the tapes now available to tourists visiting London's Guildhall.) The visits of President Kennedy and his wife to Buckingham Palace similarly brought pictures and furniture to the forefront in conversation, a stimulus that may have inspired Jacqueline Kennedy's campaign to improve the art collection of the White House. President Kennedy was an amateur painter himself and, in the matter of her own American pictures, the Queen perhaps forbore to mention that she had a portrait of Prince Charles painted by President Eisenhower.

When General de Gaulle stayed at the Palace the walls of his suite were thoughtfully decorated with French pictures, with the tactful omission, it is said, of Delaroche's *Napoleon*. But this portrait may have been avoided more in aesthetic deference to the State guest than any other reason. When President Heuss of the German Federal Republic stayed at Buckingham Palace on his State visit, he admired the pictures in the State Apartments, but asked in a puzzled way if there were no Holbeins. The Queen said little, but figuratively clapped her hands and arranged for some twenty paintings to be transported from Windsor. Then next day, as a complete surprise, she led President Heuss to the hall near his suite where the pictures had been arranged, Holbein's *Merchant of the German Steelyard*, the unobtrusively cleaned *Sir Henry Guildford*, *Derich Born*, the famous *King Henry VIII* and *Edward VI*, Durer's magnificent *Portrait of a Young Man*, Cranach's *Martin Luther*, an array of miniatures and drawings and more besides. "It was an utterly delightful surprise," Dr. Heuss said afterwards. "It was charming and most moving and showed the whole human background of the visit." Such was the auspicious overture to an evening when, for the first time for over fifty years, a German Head of State was entertained by the British Government.

When the Queen is abroad she likes to see as much of the art of a country as possible. Thus her State visit to Holland saw her at both the Gemeentemuseum and the Mauritzhaus at the Hague and at the Rijksmuseum in Amsterdam, which, as we have seen, she subsequently visited privately as soon as the chance next offered. Her Majesty's State visit to Italy similarly found her seizing the opportunity to revisit Florence; and the galleries of the Uffizi and the Accademia and the San Marco Museum were closed to the public for the day so that she might have the opportunity of enjoying their splendours without distraction. In Venice the deputy director of the civic museums, Dr. Pignatti, was surprised at the Queen's familiarity with the city until she explained she had learned it all from her pictures by Canaletto and Marco Ricci at Windsor. The pleasure of her visit to the Doge's Palace, where she saw

Tintoretto's gigantic painting of Paradise, was heightened, she explained, by the thought that at home she had her own Tintoretto pictures of the very Venetians who may have watched him at work. At worst, such compliments make for good public relations and the Queen was patently sincere. In Rome, as she moved through the crowded reception-rooms of the Quirinale, onlookers noticed her quick, all-embracing glances at the gilded and painted walls and ceiling of the glittering background. Visiting the Capitol for the mayoral reception, the Queen and Prince Philip expressed the hope that they would be able to do some sightseeing in the Capitoline Museum, and the interest they later showed in its galleries was both informed and appreciative. If Rome emotionally took her visitors to her heart, it was as much for these gestures as the radiant happiness that the Queen displayed throughout the official programme. The Queen is a good tourist, alert, interested, impressionable, with an innate capacity for collecting mementos, a characteristic perhaps inherited from Queen Alexandra, that remains unimpaired by their inevitable profusion. Thus, in India, despite the gifts showered on her, the Queen insisted on buying a naturalistic modern picture (priced at £50) which she admired while visiting the National Exhibition of Paintings in New Delhi. The theme, a rather grim study of cows eating refuse in a compound, did not seem royally promising. On the other hand, the artist, Biswanath Mukerji, had caught something of the India that the royal visitors glimpsed behind the greeting millions, the contrast of the excited crowds and, as the Queen said, "the deadpan faces of the bullocks behind them".

In an ideal world, royal tourists should no doubt become better acquainted with the arts and could afford to see less of the industries of a country. As we have remarked, the Queen is dependent on her hosts for her programme. Australia and New Zealand were notable in the concerts they arranged. Ballet or opera is included in nearly every State visit, and the Queen has seen *Peer Gynt* in Norway, *Don Carlos* in Stockholm, *Falstaff* in Rome, among others. In Nigeria the Queen genuinely welcomed the opportunity of becoming better acquainted with the arts, handcrafts and antiquities specially arrayed for her at Benin and Ibadan, and today, significantly, the Queen keeps the bronze of a negro head by the Nigerian sculptor, Ben Enwonwu, close beside her working desk as if in symbolism of her Commonwealth peoples. Mr. Enwonwu came into wide Western recognition when Epstein bought his sculpture *Yoruba Girl*; he was only in his mid-thirties when appointed art director to the Nigerian Government. When the Queen gave him a series of sittings for her portrait in bronze, he was the first sculptor of any race thus honoured. The resulting work is now in the House of Representatives at Lagos. Queen Victoria kept her Indian servants constantly at her side, but Queen Elizabeth II, content with her Enwonwu head, has drawn a wider service from the arts.

II

Even in this modern age royal patronage and diplomacy are intimately blended in their most direct transaction, as we have seen in the commissioning of gifts to the heads of other nations. When the Queen commissioned three glass goblets from Laurence Whistler for presentation to the President of France, she set more than a problem in execution and design. When completed, one goblet depicted a view of Windsor Castle, its companion showed Versailles by moonlight, while the third was suitably inscribed. The gift was a perfect evocation of the glass-worker's art, but the three glasses also needed to be cased, and Mr. C. C. Clarke, a craftsman of the Rural Industries Bureau, was accordingly called in to make a walnut cabinet in lantern style which in turn was surmounted by a silver crown worked by Leslie Durbin of the Royal College of Art. Moreover, the Queen thought the finished work so fine that she ordered six more goblets, showing all the royal residences, for ornamental display in *Britannia*. In the footsteps of Fabergé, Mr. Whistler has prepared wedding gifts for members of the Royal Family and is in a tradition of favour. But he is only one of a goodly company of artists and craftsmen who have had the stimulus and enjoyment of preparing gifts at the wish of the Queen and her husband.

The presentation to King Haakon of Norway of a painting of his yacht *Norge* by Norman Wilkinson must be judged by its suitability, for the gift passed its prime test of giving the recipient pleasure. The Queen has Wilkinson oils of her own and there is no better modern artist of the sea. The Queen dexterously blends the old and the new in her presentations to ensure the pleasurable element of surprise. On first arriving in the U.S.A. in 1957 the Queen gave a fine eighteenth-century tea-caddy, from Queen Mary's collection, to the Governor of Jamestown, and then President and Mrs. Eisenhower were presented with porcelain models of a pair of parula warblers, birds of the President's native Texas, fashioned by Dorothy Doughty, whose work in Worcester Royal porcelain is well known. Some years earlier the Queen had granted sittings to artists and colour executives of the Worcester Royal Porcelain Works for her own equestrian statuette. The Queen has similarly given a Minton dinner service to the King and Queen of Sweden, who are specially interested in ceramics, and a fine modern silver-gilt coffee set and salver were presented to the

King and Queen of Thailand on the occasion of their State visit to London.

Such courtesies oil the wheels. It long since assisted the Queen, when Sir Anthony Eden was her Prime Minister, to discover that they shared a mutual taste for Segonzac. Two Segonzac watercolours, *The Marne at Chennevières* and *Jouy en Josas* were presented to the Queen by the President of the French Republic at the time of her Coronation. It has been helpful to remember that both Mr. Vincent Massey and the former Sir David Eccles were enthusiastic collectors of Paul Nash. On the number of Churchill paintings presented to the Queen, Palace spokesmen say little. But Mr. Peter Thorneycroft, Minister of Defence, held one-man exhibitions of his paintings and completed restaurant murals of professional standard; Lord John Hope, sometime Minister of Works, painted and exhibited, and both Mr. R. A. Butler, First Secretary of State, and Dr. Beeching, head of Britain's nationalised railways, painted as a pastime. Indeed, a notable travelling exhibition could be composed solely of paintings by British politicians. The spread of artistic culture that has become a part of diplomacy is, equally, discreetly implemented by the Queen herself. Thus it was no coincidence that an exhibition of Roman drawings from Windsor was put on at the Palazzo Venezia at the time of the Queen's visit to Rome. Two years earlier the stage was similarly set for the visit of Queen Elizabeth the Queen Mother and Princess Margaret to the Eternal City by a lavish Windsor contribution of paintings, drawings, furniture and silver to an exhibition that re-created its seventeenth-century civic art. Royal treasures have never travelled farther or wider than in the present reign, now that air transport has lightened the dead weight of cartage problems. In 1962, for instance, over a hundred works from Windsor were shown in Washington and New York. Royal pictures have served to gain funds for Columbia University Scholarships and to strengthen British ties in Stockholm, Brussels, Venice, Paris, and the Hague, to name but a few of the notable exhibition stands of royal art treasures. Nor is this all. The royal yacht *Britannia* is itself used for State receptions. The royal apartments are enlivened by suitably nautical pictures by Terence Cuneo, Norman Wilkinson and others. Before the Queen first sailed abroad in the *Gothic*, she ensured that a set of characteristic English pictures were suitably displayed in the saloon, and in the same spirit a set of etchings by Alan Carr Linford — depicting Lambeth, Billingsgate and other river scenes — takes the atmosphere of England wherever *Britannia* sails.

8: THE PLEASURES OF THE QUEEN

I

The literature of the Monarchy is immense, but the personal relationship of the pen and the Crown has been an uneasy one, and has had its discords. King George III proposed a special order of knighthood for authors, and if novelists and non-fictionists cannot put K.M. after their names, in the way that artists flourish R.A., it is because such a fever of rivalry and anticipation burst around the foreshadowed Knights of Minerva that the plan was abandoned. Queen Charlotte, George III's consort, was equally courageous in appointing a novelist as her second Keeper of the Robes; and Fanny Burney for her part was surely superlative in discretion in not publishing her diary in her lifetime. One wonders what sum her journal would command today if she had lived in the age of television and headlines. One wonders, indeed, what would happen in our contemporary world if the Queen exercised her own considerable talent for authorship and published a book, perhaps a pleasant account of country life at Sandringham akin to Queen Victoria's *Leaves from a Journal of our Life in the Highlands*.

The very suggestion smacks of *lese majesté*, so high is the present-day level of respect in which the Crown is held. And yet the world of 1868 was equally set by the ears when, barely seven years after the death of her husband, Queen Victoria published what was essentially an intimate and nostalgic account of their domestic married life. What possessed her to do it? The Queen had first printed the *Leaves...* for private circulation. Naturally the book encouraged the extravagant praise of her ladies, politicians and courtiers: the Shah of Persia was so eager to read it that he had it translated into Persian, and the Queen could not resist the sense of truly personal achievement. Queen Victoria burst into public print in January 1868, and had the agreeable sensation of being the best-seller of best-sellers for the rest of the year. "People are *too kind*," she wrote, as the reverential reviews poured in. "What has she done to be so loved and liked?" A year later finds her happily receipting a cheque for royalty profits, which are said to have exceeded £30,000. "She quite approves" she wrote to Sir Theodore Martin — royal letters are usually in the third person — "of what he intends doing with the remaining £4,016. *6d.* Of this the Queen would wish him (her editor) to send her a cheque for £50, which she wished to give away. £2,516 she wishes *absolutely* to devote to *a* charity ... and the remaining £1,450 she wishes to keep for other gifts of a *charitable* nature, at least to people who are *not rich*". Encouraged by the tremendous sales, the Queen published a sequel *More Leaves...* and was deterred only with difficulty from writing a biography of her servant, John Brown. But the publication of her Letters, and further extracts from her Journals, on the express authority of King Edward VII and King George V, provided precedents that led Queen Elizabeth II to authorize the remarkably human and candid biographies of King George VI and Queen Mary, both literary milestones in the first decade of her reign. And it appears to be true that these royal yet realistic biographies illustrate the trend of the Queen's own favourite reading.

Guests invited aboard the royal yacht *Britannia* at the conclusion of an overseas tour noted the books, for example, lying on a table in her private drawing-room, Meriel Buchanan's *Queen Victoria's Relations*, Lord Grantley's *Silver Spoon*, a couple of books on Greece, A. W. Moore's *Social and*

Economic History for heavy reading, and Richard Gordon's *Doctor in the House* for light relaxation. Again, when an Australian spokesman was able to comment on the Queen's reading, he mentioned her interest in war diaries and memoirs. Her taste for current autobiography is also widely known, ranging from the best-selling account of Elsa and her lion cubs to *Grace and Favour* by Loelia, Duchess of Westminster. The Queen enjoys any professional account of her craft, and has read the Shah of Persia, King Hussein of Jordan, and Princess Wilhelmina of the Netherlands, among recent royal authors. But the Queen long since acquired the Countess Mountbatten's old habit of browsing: she is a great dipper and likes to have current books ready to hand to fill in odd minutes. Novels are in a minority because, I am told, the Queen has little real time for fiction; she has read some famed proletarian novels in order to gain a deeper understanding of life in the back-streets; she is familiar with Mary Renault's fictional reconstructions of the ancient world and has read some Laurence Durrell. Indeed, the books supplied to Buckingham Palace and Windsor Castle by Bumpus, the royal booksellers, are extraordinarily varied and do not exclude paperbacks.

In literature, as in nearly every other field, the Queen has, needless to say, her own unique viewpoint. It was founded on the days of her girlhood when the Royal Library at Windsor, with its shining cabinets, laden bookshelves and railed balconies, offered a peaceful, studious and yet enticing atmosphere. The Royal Library is a treasure house: it has two unique specimens of the press of Caxton as well as the manuscript of Mozart's first oratorio and the second folio Shakespeare read by Charles I while imprisoned in Carisbrooke, and inscribed by him "While there's life, there's hope". Yet the library is also the royal circulating library of the Royal Family and their households; it is concerned with the everyday commerce of literature as well as with the preservation of the Shah Jehan Nameh, a rarity of Persian illumination dating from the days of the Moguls. The Royal Library was founded when William IV found himself the only Sovereign in Europe without such a luxury and decided to establish a library in what had been Queen Elizabeth I's bedroom. (Her ghost still reputedly walks there.) But there are also treasures from the earlier libraries of George III and George IV, the Mentz Psalter of 1457, a Faust and Schoffer German Bible of 1462, supreme among the examples of early printing, and Henry VIII's tract against Luther. If the Queen wished she could also send for signed presentation copies dating from Boswell's *Life of Johnson* — with a long inscription by the author to King George III — down via Dickens, Thackeray, Stevenson, Kipling, Hardy, Robert Bridges, Galsworthy, Barrie, and Maugham to the present day. It is tempting to suppose that the Queen in childhood may have read Masefield's *Reynard the Fox*, with drawings by the author on nearly every page, and her grandfather's inscription, "This book was illustrated for me by the Poet Laureate himself. G.R.I." But probably such books were not handled, even on Sundays. One book at Windsor, a copy of Scott's *Peveril of the Peak*, is seldom handled at all, if it can be avoided. For it has been inscribed in Queen Victoria's hand, "This book was read, up to the mark in Page 81, to my beloved Husband during his fatal illness." The signed presentation copies are moreover still accumulating. The Queen makes a general rule not to accept gifts from those whom she does not know personally, but this ordinance is viewed liberally in the case of authors. Over four hundred such gifts, "with humble duty", have been accepted thus far in her reign, giving many modern writers the comforting assurance of at least some attention from posterity.

The Queen had a girlhood passion for poetry and is thought to have written verse herself. She dutifully read most of Dickens and the Brontë sisters, a great deal of Scott and Thackeray, Wells, Shaw and other standards. But perhaps the Queen's literary acquaintance is also shown by a private library room in the Clarence Tower where some four hundred volumes of the Queen's earlier books have been arranged. This establishes that in her twenties the Queen had read some of the Studio books on modern design and many of the Batsford books on the British Heritage; she owned Clough Williams-Ellis's *On Trust for the Nation* and the four volumes of the Quennells' *History of Everyday Things in England*, and G. M. Trevelyan's *English Social History*. There were reference books such as *The Scottish Clans and Their Tartans* by Innes of Learney, the *Scottish Country Dance Book*, and the librettos of the Savoy Operas side by side with N. R. Wilkinson's two volumes on the Wilton House pictures. The Queen practised French by reading Molière, did not cross the Atlantic before reading William McFee's *Sir Martin Frobisher*, and indeed did not take up thoroughbred breeding without consulting *The Authentic Arabian Horse* by Lady Wentworth.

On more formal shelves, the Queen cherishes two little volumes in green leather of the poems of Dante Gabriel Rossetti, the seven volumes of *Pocket Poets*, the poetical works of Whittier and *The Arabian Nights*. But there is also a copy of *The Seven Pillars of Wisdom* with her own cypher in gold, the six volumes of Churchill's *World Crisis*, together with Pepys, Omar Khayyam, and the *Pilgrim's Progress*. These are the books one might find in any comfortable English home, but add *Helvellyn to Himalaya* by Spencer Chapman, one or two old thrillers of

Buchan, Viscount Samuel's *Memoirs* and the naval memoirs of Sir Roger Keyes, *The Crock of Gold* by James Stephens, Eric Parker's *Surrey* and the book of drawings of bombed London by Hanslip Fletcher. Noted down, jumbled, as one finds them on the shelves, these nevertheless afford the evidence of an orderly and well-stocked mind. The Queen has some exceptional treasures. To a nurse she once handed a gardening book which had belonged to Florence Nightingale, and who but a Queen would have a copy of A. A. Milne's *When We Were Very Young* inscribed by an Archbishop of York? The Queen also personally possesses a first edition of *Through the Looking Glass*, and a book of poems that once belonged to Thomas Gray. But among her more intimate books one can also find MacQueen-Pope's history of Drury Lane Theatre, Lorene Squire's *Wild Fowling with a Camera*, *The Glass of Fashion* by Ira Norris and Laurette Cope, an account of the Flying Doctor service of Australia and a *History of the 7th Argylls*, some of Alison Uttley's country books, Hudson Moore's monograph on old glass and, unexpectedly, Feilden's *Anglice Recipe Book*, the *Book of Good Housekeeping* and *The Gold Cook Book* by L. P. de Gouy. The Queen's intent study of everything to be covered in official duties is shown by a planning report on London schools, a book of ballet education, A. E. Pavey's *Story of the Growth of Nursing*, and even a pronouncing dictionary of Gaelic. There are, too, travel books ranging over Holland, Poland, Tasmania, Ottawa, India ... books constantly replaced by newcomers.

Royal dinner-table conversation often runs over current publishing. On one occasion, when Cecil Woodham-Smith's *The Reason Why* was discussed, its basic theme of the Crimean War was enacted afterwards in a charade and quickly dismissed as too easy. The Queen enjoys local history and is susceptible to books of Scottish topography. Such studies as Dixon Scott's *Scottish Counties* and Arthur Gardner's book on the Western Highlands show the usage of regular handling. Among the Queen's innumerable art books are such odd bedfellows as the *Paintings of Elioth Gruner*, and the *Decorative Art of Leon Bakst*, at the opposite poles of twentieth-century graphic design. But they have been read and used, and bespeak a catholicity of outlook and imagination.

Some years ago, somewhat to his annoyance, a camera was turned in close-up on Prince Philip's naval desk to reveal that his casual reading at that time was concerned with Arthur Koestler's *Thieves in the Night*, Phyllis Bottome's *The Mortal Storm*, and *P.Q.17* by Godfrey Winn. When Neil Morris designed the panelling and fitments of Prince Philip's bedroom he received instructions that at least sixteen yards of shelf space for books should be built in. But no one is conspicuously better off for this information. A list of books on an overseas royal train similarly showed only the verdict of a selection committee and not the Queen's own choice. The Palace authorities are rightly chary of releasing details of the Queen's immediate reading. When she can relax from official papers she reads to please herself and, as a Sunday newspaper has observed, it is not part of her Sovereign role to be a fiction critic for the nation.

II

In music the Queen is curiously representative of her generation. In girlhood she studied under Miss Mabel Lander, who incidentally had also taught Sir Malcolm Sargent, and she was an attentive and persevering pupil. Her father was filled with glowing pride when he first heard her performance of a concert piece at Windsor and confided to Miss Lander he had no idea the Princess could have been taught so much in the time. But lessons ceased at eighteen when she was playing Beethoven, Chopin, and Debussy, not plodding merely through the easier movements but playing, as her teacher said, very well indeed and with real musical feeling. The Queen still enjoys the piano but nowadays finds she has little time to spare as a musician. Although there is a piano in the royal apartments aboard the *Britannia*, as if ready to fill the leisure hours of a cruise, a member of the Royal Household tells me he has seldom seen the Queen near it. The lighter long-play records of musical shows were more in evidence, with the orchestral medleys known as mood music, yet Mozart operas were also heard, and when Her Majesty visited Glyndebourne privately to see *The Marriage of Figaro* she admitted that it was one of her favourites at home. Much-played recordings, however, also range from Gilbert and Sullivan to Elgar's *Dream of Gerontius*; the Queen has a penchant for choral music, as she has for the much lighter airs of military ceremonial. Three much-thumbed volumes of Beethoven's Sonatas are often in evidence when she is attracted to the piano, but she has also sometimes bent an attentive ear and eye to the airs of *Let's Make an Opera* by Benjamin Britten.

An idiosyncratic tinge of classicism was instilled in her musical taste in the days of the Windsor madrigals, when Eton boys and occasionally the Eton choir came to encourage the two Princesses in the enjoyment of singing. Their authentic pleasure was marked by the volumes of madrigals among the Princess Elizabeth's wedding gifts, and her considerable knowledge in the specialized field of choral music was shown by her choice of a little-known Parry anthem for her wedding, with the Orlando Gibbons's *Amen* and Crimond's less usual version of *The Lord's My Shepherd*. On the eve of the wedding, the choir could not get the descant right and the bride was heard humming it over to Dr. William McKie, the Westminster Abbey organist, to indicate precisely how she wished it to be heard. The music of the Coronation, equally, will long be remembered; but few realize that it introduced eight new choral pieces and indeed included, at the Queen's direct wish, more new music and revised arrangements than in any previous Coronation. The cherished glories of musical tradition still remained, the setting of *Zadok the Priest* that Handel composed for George III, Parry's entrance anthem, *I was glad*, Stanford's *Gloria in Excelsis*… But the Homage anthem *O Lord Our Governor* by Healey Willan of Toronto was the first example of Coronation music ever contributed by the Dominions. Dr. Vaughan Williams made a new arrangement of the Old Hundredth and a motet for the Communion; Sir Arnold Bax composed a Coronation March and Sir Arthur Bliss a Processional. Sir William Walton's *Orb and Sceptre* was played before the service and he composed the *Te Deum*, while the *Creed* and *Sanctus* were from Vaughan Williams's great *Mass in G Minor*.

This alternating simplicity and splendour was indeed emblematic of the Queen. She remembers that Purcell was once an Abbey organist, she enjoys Byrd, and as Patron of the Bach Choir she has demonstrated on more than one occasion that she likes what she knows, but that her knowledge is wide. Among the recognized favourites of the Queen are Jeremiah Clarke's *Trumpet Voluntary*, Purcell's *Airs on Trumpet Tunes* and Handel's *Water Music*. These have a ceremonial ring, but for concerts at the Royal Festival Hall, when a programme has been arranged in part to her choosing, Her Majesty has also signified her preference for such works as Elgar's *Cockaigne* overture, Vaughan Williams's *Sea Symphony* … sturdy, unshocking stuff that sometimes contains a hint to professional musicians of a compassionate royal wish to ease rehearsals. The Queen greatly enjoyed "a splendid performance" of the Schumann *Piano Concerto in A Minor* given by the remarkable Michael Roll when he was still only 15. But if the Queen does not often attend concerts privately it is because music cannot offer complete relaxation when she knows, as Dorothy Laird has said, that even when the house lights are down her faintly-seen face and silhouette are being studied on all sides.

In far lighter vein, the Queen does not closely follow the constantly changing world of "pops". She prefers "trad" and "oldie" dance music during the impromptu dances held at Windsor and Sandringham, particularly in the rather sweet, swinging style. The millions who also enjoy music while they work are not remote in spirit from the Queen, for she often listens to the distant mid-morning music of the band during the Changing of the Guard in the forecourt at Buckingham Palace, and finds it a pleasant background accompaniment of her working hours.

The Queen is Patron of the Royal Academy of Music, the British Federation of Music Festivals, the Edinburgh Festival, the Royal Amateur Orchestral Society, and the Royal Scottish Country Dance Society, among musical duties that, as she invariably likes to make clear to organizers and sponsors, are never a chore. Before she came to the Throne, as we have already seen, she seldom missed presenting the annual awards at the Royal College of Music, was regularly present at the Windsor Festival of Church Music, and quietly attended an occasional recital at the Wigmore Hall, apart from the more formal occasions at the larger concert halls. As Queen, her first royal concert at the Royal Festival Hall was adeptly staged to aid the Musicians' Benevolent Fund, and this is a cause she notably likes to help by giving her attendance at a concert every two or three years. It should be mentioned, too, that a major gesture to musical scholarship was achieved when she presented the Royal Music Library to the British Museum. This occurred just two centuries after George II had presented the Museum with the library of royal books collected by the Kings of England up to that time. The Queen's gift consisted of over 7,000 pieces of music, including 97 volumes of autograph works by Handel. The accumulation had, it is true, been on loan to the Museum for nearly fifty years, but the collection on the market could have cost the Museum thousands of pounds.

III

The Queen is only an occasional opera-goer. Something must suffer: she cannot do everything in her unusually busy life. Opera in her reign got off to a false start by the inappropriate staging of *Gloriana*, Benjamin Britten's study of the ageing Elizabeth I, for the Coronation gala performance. Nevertheless, the traditional glitter of opera at Covent Garden has memorably hallmarked many State visits; and the festivities have been ornamented, while avoiding the banal, with productions of *Le Coq d'Or*, *The Bartered Bride* and Bellini's *La Sonnambula*. The Queen was raptly introduced to *La Bohème* in her teens; and she has also had experience abroad of *Peer Gynt* in the National Theatre of Oslo, scenes from *Don Carlos* in Stockholm and Verdi's *Falstaff* — with Tito Gobbi in the name role — in Rome. She has watched special performances of opera and ballet in the Sao Carlos Opera House in Lisbon, at the Paris Opera and in the little long-forgotten opera-house of Louis XV at Versailles and the even stranger Drottingham Theatre in Sweden, where a perfect eighteenth-century theatre,

153

closed and in darkness for a century, has come to renewed life like a twentieth-century sleeping beauty. The Queen has similarly seen *The Magic Flute* and paid her lighter respects to Gilbert and Sullivan by attending D'Oyly Carte performances of *The Mikado* and *Ruddigore*, as well as a student production of *Iolanthe* and Tyrone Guthrie's production of *H.M.S. Pinafore*. She has heard Callas sing and once went privately to Covent Garden to hear Boris Christoff in *Boris Godunov*. Perhaps her most memorable operatic experience, however, was also the least expected. It occurred in mid-morning when the Queen was visiting La Scala in Milan and expected to see only the museum and the empty auditorium. Instead she discovered the full orchestra in its place, the lights were dimmed, the curtains rose and disclosed the stage set for the second act of *Lucia di Lammermoor*. For twelve minutes of enchantment the Australian soprano, Joan Sutherland, sang the beautiful duet with Gianni Raimondi, the tenor, while the Queen and her party listened in delight in the empty opera house. This rendition on the part of La Scala was surely a gesture surpassing any bouquet.

The Queen is not a balletomane and yet enjoys ballet. The creation of the Royal Ballet under a royal charter, which was among the early artistic landmarks of her reign, implied more than the amalgamation of the Covent Garden and Sadler's Wells ballet companies. The former Wells school became the Royal Ballet school and the pressing difficulty of accommodating one hundred boarders from the British Isles and the Commonwealth was solved by the leasing of White Lodge in Richmond Park from the Crown. This was the first married home of the Queen's parents and originally intended as the prospective birthplace of their first child, the Queen herself. But it had proved too awkwardly located for amenable royal living and the Queen's proposal for the ballet school settled a two-way problem. Close to the room in which Nelson sketched the battle-plan of Trafalgar with a finger dipped in wine, young dancers trace more intricate patterns in ballet shoes. The gracious atmosphere is essential to their years of tuition and the Crown Commissioners are relieved of a property that was long among their more onerous responsibilities. This can be counted one of the Queen's good deeds by stealth, and her presence at Sadler's Wells for the twenty-fifth anniversary ballet was similarly a mark of recognition of no less firm and deliberate intention.

The Queen has watched the dancing of Dame Margot Fonteyn, Moira Shearer, Beryl Grey, Pamela May, Julia Farron, Michael Somes, John Hart, Leslie Edwards and many others. She saw Ulanova — "A most beautiful performance I shall always remember" — when the Bolshoi Ballet appeared at Covent Garden in 1956. Gala evenings of ballet in the presence of the Queen tend to be broken into extracts, the more sparkling moments of *Les Rendezvous*, *Coppelia*, *Cinderella* and so forth, but the Queen first went to the ballet when she was only seventeen, and has stocked her memory with a wide repertoire that includes *The Firebird*, *Les Sylphides*, *Gaete Parisienne* and *Ondine*. Indeed, the Queen has frequently shown the impetuous enthusiasm of any ballet-lover, and she once went twice within a month to see *The Sleeping Beauty*, and has twice seen Nureyev in *Giselle*.

IV

A leading player upon the world's stage, the Queen's interest in the theatre tends to be semi-professional. As with her own Sovereign role, the stage uses music, pageantry, costume, scenery, lighting, acting and diction. The dimming of the lights in the House of Lords before the Queen enters for the State

Opening of Parliament is sheer theatrecraft, and the Queen echoes Elizabeth I's sympathy for players, for she, too, knows what it is to be the constant focus of an audience. When the Queen attended the Old Vic's first night of *Henry VIII* a few weeks before her Coronation, the House of Tudor and the House of Windsor were curiously linked in the traffic of the stage. When in the last scene the King asked Archbishop Cranmer the name of the royal baby and was told "Elizabeth", an extra in the stage crowd happened to murmur "And a very nice name, too!" and by a freak of acoustics his words echoed round the theatre, causing a storm of applause. The tribute linked the Queen with the humblest of her players. In her Accession year, when *The Young Elizabeth* was staged at the New Theatre, with Mary Morris as the Princess, the Queen saw it twice within a month. Earlier, when in celebration of her twentieth birthday she arranged one of the first theatre parties of her very own, she booked seats for Robert Morley and Wendy Hiller in *The First Gentleman* and, after watching this re-enactment of family history, expressed pleasure that the portrayal was so "true to life".

Plaintive voices are sometimes raised that the Queen's taste in the theatre is lightweight rather than serious, that she prefers to be entertained rather than to be informed and does not eagerly seek out sermons in kitchen sinks. It is admittedly strange that in the native land of Shakespeare the most publicized theatrical event of the year in which the Royal Family are concerned should be a Royal Variety Performance, but no stranger than that the annual Royal Film Performance — in aid of the British Cinematograph Trade Benevolent Fund — should be so often devoted to American films. But we are fond of admitting ourselves a strange nation. Until *The Merchant of Venice* was given at Windsor in 1905, no reigning monarch had sat right through a Shakespeare play for eighty years. The Queen has seen *King Lear*, *As You Like It*, *Romeo and Juliet* and several of the historical plays, and her dramatic acquaintance ranges over Marlowe and Molière, Congrave and Sheridan to Christopher Fry and Anouilh. Given the choice of three plays when a visit to the Chichester Festival Theatre was being planned, she decided against a Restoration adaptation of John Fletcher's much rewritten comedy *The Chances* and the heavy going of John Ford's *The Broken Heart* and chose *Uncle Vanya*. Many discerning playgoers would agree with her taste, and Her Majesty's immediate notice of a new theatre was true patronage. The fact that the Queen has seen T. S. Eliot's *The Confidential Clerk*, *The Summer of the Seventeenth Doll* and the C.P. Snow–Ronald Millar play *The Affair* should dispose of the charge that the intelligent theatre receives no support in high places. The Queen saw Peter Ustinov's *Romanoff and Juliet*, Edith Evans and Sybil Thorndike in *The Chalk Garden*, and she has been diverted by Rattigan pieces as varied as *The Sleeping Princess* and *Separate Tables*. Yet these plays reflect the Queen's interest, for she has often demonstrated that she turns to the theatre for relaxation and entertainment and never for prosaic duty. M. Jean Chauvel, the French ambassador, struck her taste perfectly when he hit upon a new idea in diplomatic interchanges and took her as his guest to see Anouilh's *L'Invitation au Chateau* in its original French. When the Compagnie Madeleine Renault-Jean Louis Barrault was in London, and the directors sent the Queen a choice of plays, they had anticipated that she would select *Le Misanthrope*. Instead she chose *Occupe-toi d'Amelie*, the farce of which her grandfather had blushingly written, "The hottest thing I ever saw on the stage". But the Queen merely said, "It plays much better than it reads."

We sometimes see the musical comedies patronized by the Queen listed accusingly, as if gaiety should be frowned upon in queens, but how stuffy she might seem if she had ignored *Guys and Dolls*, *Call Me Madam*, *West Side Story*, *Salad Days*, *My Fair Lady*, and *Sail Away*. One tends to forget that King George V saw *Rose Marie* four times and the first all-black written and performed American ragtime musical In Dahomey was performed at Buckingham Palace. It is on record that the Queen's grandfather went to the theatre one hundred and seventy times in the course of his reign and he once carried his zeal to the length of six shows in a month. But he always insisted on cricking his neck in a box rather than sit in the stalls. In 1928, when George V and Queen Mary went to see *The Trial of Mary Dugan*, and there were no boxes in the theatre, a special box had to be built at great expense in the middle of the dress circle in order that royal etiquette might be observed.

In contrast, our present Queen sat in the 10*s*. stalls when she saw a similar play, Agatha Christie's *Witness for the Prosecution* acted by John Counsell's repertory company at the Theatre Royal, Windsor, and the Queen so enjoyed the cosy atmosphere of the little theatre, just below the Castle, that she booked thirty seats for the revue *The World's the Limit* the following month and took along her entire Ascot houseparty. A few months later the Queen was there again with her mother and sister to see an advance production of *Grab Me a Gondola*. In 1957 Mr. Counsell offered the Queen the use of the entire theatre for a night in Ascot week, when Michael Brett's comedy *Four in Hand* was being presented. The Queen accepted this handsome gesture and the 500 seats were filled with her guests, the staff of the Castle and their friends. But the Queen prefers to pay for her seats and a block booking of thirty-five seats in the balcony stalls was made when she subsequently took her Ascot guests to see *Sabrina Fair*. On other occasions, the Queen's choice has fallen on *Jane Eyre* and *You Never Can Tell*. Times were in earlier reigns when command performances were held at Windsor Castle itself, with cast, costumes and scenery transported by special trains at some expense. (The Edwardian bill for an evening of Sutro at Sandringham was £233. 14*s*. 6*d*., when the sovereign was worth a true twenty shillings.) But to the players there was always an atmosphere, an aftertaste, of champagne and cold pie in the Steward's Room around these performances. Scene-cloths and battens had to be hung without marking walls or ceilings, productions had to be frantically cut down to size and playing under nightmarish conditions to an unusually small but exceptionally exalted audience was invariably, to the actors, an ordeal imposing great strain. Since 1926 only two full-scale productions have been transported to Windsor. This was during the war, when performances of Firth Shepherd's *Up and Doing* and George Black's *Black Vanities* gave the companies a brief respite from the blitz. Buckingham Palace has been occasioned no flurry of second thoughts by the appearance of a Shakespeare company, the Pablo Casals concert and other recitals at the White House. Noted by Sir Frederick Ponsonby, the cautionary tale is still told of the Italian tenor at Windsor who sang with such power that he made Queen Victoria's white lace cap flutter as if in a gale.

In patronizing her local repertory company at Windsor, Queen Elizabeth sets a good example to theatregoers. She has similarly recognized and implemented the amateur theatre, both by going to see *The Frog* at the Scala, which Princess Margaret was concerned in producing with a group of friends, and by attending the York mystery plays, among other productions. While staying in Sussex with her friends, Lord and Lady Rupert Nevill, the Queen not infrequently went into Brighton for a show at the Theatre Royal. On one occasion Her Majesty is said to have queued unrecognized with her hosts while waiting to enter the theatre and, one Saturday night, the thriller *Write Me a Murder* was doing such good business that the royal party of eight had to split up and sit in two separate rows.

The Queen has, in fact, enhanced the dignity of the theatre and diminished none of her own by playgoing frequently and habitually. Making up her mind on the spur of the moment that she would like to see *The Reluctant Debutante*, she accepted seats at the very side of the circle, an experience known to every last-minute playgoer, and she sat in the back row to see Trevor Howard in *Two Stars For Comfort*. Offered Row M at the Haymarket for *Lady Windermere's Fan*, the Queen commented, "I don't mind where I sit as long as I can see and hear." But what a difference this is from the formality of royal theatregoing in former days.

The Queen usually books her seats through Ashton & Mitchell, who were allowed to style themselves the "Royal Agency" in Edward VII's reign and now hold a Royal Warrant of the present reign. The original Mitchell was a Bond Street bookseller who sold opera tickets to Queen Victoria the year before she came to the Throne, and Ashton joined the firm in 1872 when only nineteen and soon captured the Prince of Wales's custom. When Queen Victoria went to Her Majesty's Theatre one evening it was carefully recorded that her party arrived in nine carriages, complete with gentlemen ushers, Pages of Honour and a Captain of the Yeomen of the Guard. Dangerously, the Queen was led to her box by officials carrying lighted wax tapers and walking backwards. When our own Queen went to see Sir Alec Guinness in *Ross* at the

Haymarket, she arrived by taxi — and the Queen often takes her seat in a theatre so inconspicuously that the audience are unaware of her presence. King George VI undramatically established a precedent as the first monarch to sit with his people in this way when he went to the Strand Theatre to see Harry Green in *Fifty-Fifty* and the management had no appropriate boxes to offer. In those days it was always possible for a manager to tell by security precautions when royalty was expected. Though no less strong, security today is so inconspicuous that when the Queen went to the Duchess Theatre to see Agatha Christie's play *The Unexpected Guest* the box office knew nothing of her intentions until she entered the theatre. The seats had been booked in another name. When the Queen patronized another thriller, *The Big Killing*, the management were told of her coming only twenty minutes before the curtain rose. In this case four people in Row G were quietly asked if they would agree to seating elsewhere … and only the previous evening the Queen had been to see the irreverent revue *Beyond the Fringe*, with its quiet mockery of the established institutions and even of the Queen herself. The show was not altered in any way because of Her Majesty's presence. As Peter Cook, one of the four-man cast, said afterwards, "We thought the best thing to do was to ignore her, in the politest possible way, of course."

The Queen is an escapist playgoer, finding in light comedies, such as *The Grass Is Greener* and Noël Coward's *Nude With Violin*, the refreshing release from environment which has always been a function of the theatre. When a show particularly entertains her, she likes to convey her enjoyment to others. Thus she saw Lionel Bart's *Oliver* while Prince Philip was abroad, and then returned three weeks later with a party that included her husband and Lord and Lady Rupert Nevill.

Similarly, Her Majesty saw *The Bride Comes Back* during its Brighton production and saw it again in London when she took the present Duke and Duchess of Kent to the theatre as part of the evening to celebrate their engagement.

The Queen has sat in the second row of the circle; she has never been known to be late, but, when she once arrived just as the house lights were being lowered, the royal party groped their way to their seats so hurriedly that they were halfway along the aisle before the manager could catch up with them. This increasing informality led one night to the inevitable moment when the royal group sat in the wrong seats and had to be asked to move up two.

The Queen took it in good part. After the show, as others have noted, she is always appreciative and understanding in her comments, and does not overlook the small part players. Indeed, the Queen is so attentive to those who entertain her that, after the Windsor Rep. production of *You Never Can Tell*, she said that she had specially noticed a young actor who, in fact, had walked on as a waiter and had not spoken a line. Appreciation could not go farther.

V

On a Saturday night at Sandringham in 1906 King Edward VII listened by telephone to Melba singing at Covent Garden and when the "articulation of the artistes" grew too muffled, he asked to be connected by the electrophone service to the operetta *See-See* and pronounced it wonderful. More than half a century later his great-granddaughter shares the enjoyment of her subjects when she watches television, but for the Queen the pleasure is enhanced by not being a central participant in the scene. The arts of television have established a curious new link between the Crown and the people. The TV announcer does not bow before he begins reading the news. The man in the street may be interviewed for television unaware that the Queen may be looking and listening. The Queen may tune in a programme such as *Z Cars*, which is fiction based on the facts of a provincial policeman's existence, and the fictitious episodes are enhanced for the Queen by seeming to bring her close to the realism of everyday existence in a manner impossible in the age of George V.

Whenever television notables meet the Queen they find her closely conversant with the programmes. They know that, from time to time, she watches the London magazine features such as *Tonight* and *Monitor*, enjoys programmes of mingled music and ballet, will occasionally "take in" a Western, but she skips the serials and seldom follows the weekly magazine programmes on international affairs involving current topics on which she is too well versed already. The Queen enjoys a good play, but it has been explained that many demand too much of the precious commodity she can least spare: her time. At the same time the Queen can leave a televised play for a few minutes and then pick it up again in a way denied to her in the theatre.

Some of the shorter play series are therefore the most appealing. *Maigret*, the Pinto spy series, *Brothers-in-Law* and other half-hour plays have gained royal attention. A series of Canadian plays much interested the Queen when shown by the B.B.C. and she occasionally looks at *What's My Line*. She watched some of the episodes of the Churchill war series *The Valiant Years*, but here again the demands of a twenty-six-part series conflicted with precious minutes and the Queen, like many of us, caught up with some episodes only on the second time round, some not at all. The news service of television is of value to the Queen: while watching Prince Philip play polo she also kept an eye on the televised racing. When Pat Smythe won the Queen Elizabeth Cup at the Horse of the Year show, a telephone message from the Queen to the arena disclosed that she had been looking-in. Though she does not see many commercial programmes, inquiries were made on her behalf to discover whether a certain episode of *Wagon Train* would be repeated. By and large the Queen also enjoys travel films and documentaries. An American series looking back over the past sixty years greatly interested her. She saw the first, dealing with the pre-1914 period, but then missed *The Jazz Age* and *VE Plus Ten* and asked if these sequels could be screened at Sandringham. The Queen also expressed a desire to see the Malcolm Muggeridge programme *The Thirties*, but unluckily in this instance the different tracks of the sound and vision system did not fit the Sandringham projectors.

Films beyond count have, however, flickered at Sandringham and Balmoral since the night of novelty at the turn of the century when George V, then Prince of Wales, wrote in a letter, "After dinner last night we had the Biograph or moving pictures in the ballroom. Some of them were marvellously good." Three years earlier, however, in the Green Drawing Room at Windsor, Queen Victoria had watched the "Cinematograph representing parts of my Jubilee Procession, and various other things. They are wonderful, but I thought them a little hazy and rather too rapid in their movements."

Today Queen Elizabeth II may have the same reservations for some of the travelogues, racing and nature films she has also produced herself. Victoria and Albert were both enthusiastically interested in photography and became patrons of the newly-formed Photographic Society as early as 1853. Our present Queen, we may recall, innocently commenced the first day of her reign taking animal shots from the balcony of

Treetops, the forest hotel in Kenya, and a film producer lunching at Buckingham Palace some years later found her well versed in professional phraseology. The Queen always takes her movie camera overseas and wields it personally, regardless of watching crowds. Unlike her husband, however, the Queen has never permitted her films to be widely seen. The titles of the motion pictures shown to her privately are also not announced. But they include a score or so of the year's best films, Italian and French — and on occasion Japanese and Indian — as well as British and American. The Queen asked to have *The Dawn*, a documentary about Ghana, shown to her at Balmoral, and a short film made in Sweden, *Fiddler's Highway*, was also included in the programme. Her Majesty has also similarly seen one of the films that Harold Lloyd based on his old silent comedies. Both at Buckingham Palace and Clarence House, private theatres enable the royal ladies to suit precisely their own taste in arranging showings for themselves and their friends.

The annual royal film premieres, held to benefit the Cinematograph Trade Benevolent Fund, reflect royal taste only when the organizing selection committee contrives to submit an alternative choice to the Palace. There was a time when cinema publicists attempted to call this a film command performance, only to incur a rebuke from Palace officials. There was a time, indeed, when King George VI was thoroughly angry at finding the crowds so ill controlled that he and his Consort had practically to push their way through a narrow avenue across the pavement. The present Queen patiently sat through a mediocre American musical *Because You're Mine* in her Accession Year, a poorish Walt Disney, *Rob Roy*, in her Coronation year, but she is said to have been displeased by the villainous presentation of the Prince Regent in *Beau Brummell*. Hitchcock's *To Catch a Thief* and the Rank naval war film *The Battle of the River Plate* were presented to better effect in successive years. After the presentation of *Les Girls* in 1957, and the publicity jostling of some of the so-called stars presented after the performance, it was announced that the Queen's presence in future years could not be taken for granted. However, the breach was healed and Her Majesty attended the premiere of *West Side Story* in 1962. Her presence was similarly signified for *Richard III*, *Dunkirk* and *The Guns of Navarone*, among other premieres for charity. On at least two occasions the Queen has also privately visited the London Casino to sample the big screen stereoscopic wonders of Cinerama. Strangely enough, one evening, the row behind the Queen was occupied by some thirty Soviet transport workers who were there as guests of their British colleagues. The Queen quietly entered the theatre just as the lights dimmed, but still in time to be recognized by some of the Russians, several of whom rose to their feet until the Queen's hostess, Lady Brabourne, signalled to them to remain seated. This was before the visit to Britain of Mr. Khrushchev and Marshal Bulganin, and thus, on a June evening in a London theatre, flimsy strands of coincidence first bridged the gulf of nearly forty years between Ekaterinburg and Windsor.

9: THE QUEEN AND THE PORTRAITISTS

I

In the first decade of her reign the Queen sat to twenty artists for thirty-two portraits. These included the special sittings she gave for the correct delineation of four pictures of royal ceremonial, but not the time allotted for five or six equestrian portraits. In addition, the Queen sat to two sculptors, including six sittings at the Kensington studio of Sir Charles Wheeler, President of the Royal Academy. In one busy year the Queen sat for seven portraits and the following year she sat to six different artists, for four of whom the honour of a royal portrait was a novel and no doubt nerve-wracking experience. On average the Queen gave one hundred and eighty sittings, an involvement in ten years of between two and three hundred hours of her time. This gives us some measure of the role that portraiture still plays in projecting and enhancing the royal image, a permanent emphasis of sovereignty no less important amid the transience of this television age than in all the reigns of the past four hundred years.

In all but twelve of her portraits the Queen is depicted in evening dress. Apart from the State Portrait in Coronation robes, there are two pictures portraying the Queen in uniform and four in the mantles or robes of the paramount orders of knighthood. When films have fallen to powder, when photographs have been retouched and reprinted beyond all semblance of truth, the oil paintings will remain, the Queen full length or three-quarter length, standing or seated, more than thirty portraits so far seen through twenty pairs of eyes, all

167

widely different, but all with their subtle resemblances, portraits, however, that all agree in showing not a person but a Queen.

The average man or woman cannot sit to an artist without a measure of gratification and even affectation, but not the Queen. Long ago, in her girlhood, it was gently impressed on her that artists wished to paint her because she was a Princess and not merely because she was pretty. More than the camera, the artist's canvas is still one of the accessories of her royal profession in making her known to her people. Most of the Queen's subjects will do no more than glimpse her once or twice in a lifetime. The portrait presents the durable embodiment bathed in the eternal light of art. This significant truth is seen in the State Portrait, painted once in a reign shortly after the Coronation, commissioned by the Government from a leading artist of the day, once copied by him and then more widely reproduced, both manually and by mechanical process, for distribution to the major Embassies abroad and other Government buildings overseas. It thus highlights the sovereignty of the Queen and magnifies her personality, an iconographic emblem of the whole era. The State Portraits of Edward VII and George V by Luke Fildes in Buckingham Palace, and Sir Gerald Kelly's State Portrait of King George VI in the Crimson Drawing Room at Windsor, all seem as representative of their age as each monarch himself, though the trappings of monarchy, the ceremonial robes and costume, essentially remain the same.

II

The State Portrait of the Queen by James Gunn hangs in public view in St. George's Hall at Windsor Castle, where it has replaced the tapestry of the Castle and park landscape made for the jubilee of King George V. The commission came to the Scottish painter through the Ministry of Works appropriately in time to form a sixtieth birthday tribute, but honours garlanded the artist that year, for he had been elected president of the Royal Society of Portrait Painters that same week and he had become an Associate of the Royal Academy three months before. His earlier portrait of the Queen, in evening gown and white fur, commissioned by the Royal Regiment of Artillery, was in time to form a central feature of the Coronation summer show at the Royal Academy. Mr. Gunn was however no newcomer to royal portraiture. He had painted King George VI in 1944 and his Consort, the Queen Mother, in 1946. His original study for his famous conversation piece of Hilaire Belloc, Chesterton, and Maurice Baring had hung like a benison beside the fireplace at Clarence House when the present Queen was still Princess Elizabeth. The demands of the State Portrait nevertheless found the artist working under a sense of pressure and passing time and not without some impression of watchful posterity.

The Queen sat to Mr. Gunn, wearing her Coronation gown, Orders and jewels, during the summer recess of 1953 at Balmoral. The formal nature of the portrait required a standing pose, sometimes through most of the two-hour session, and this she endured most amiably, but Mr. Gunn was also treated as a guest at the Castle, free to watch the Queen as he pleased, with every opportunity for catching and sketching her habitual expression. Subsequently he worked in London, with the robes on a stand, and since the State Portrait must traditionally show St. Edward's Crown and the Sceptre, these priceless pieces of the Regalia arrived in their leather cases at his studio every day from the Tower of London. The task profoundly occupied the artist for six months. Eight feet high, his picture is still the largest portrait of the Queen ever painted. It was still unfinished and the artist was notably dissatisfied with the head when Mr. Laib photographed the painting at the Palace and the time came for its display at the 1954 summer exhibition at the Royal Academy. The immediate result made a Roman holiday for the critics, many of whom judged the portrait as a finished work. They found the nose too prominent, the neck too long. One critic asserted that diamonds, silks, velvet, even skin and hair, all had the insipid texture of linoleum. Seen through the haze of lingering Coronation enchantment, some thought it a pity that the portrait was unsmiling, which provoked Gunn to retort that what some people wanted was "a grinning picture showing all the Queen's teeth". The Queen gave further sittings the following year, on returning from Australia, so that the portrait might be completed to the artist's satisfaction. But her *aide memoir* system as always worked perfectly and, according to report, the Queen greeted the artist with a mischievous smile, "Now, Mr. Gunn, with teeth or without?"

The master copy of the improved portrait was displayed by the Royal Society of Portrait Painters in 1956. Now the Queen was pictured wearing her "postage-stamp" coronet of cross and rose-sprays instead of being bare-headed, and the face was shown slightly fuller, the eyes softer, and the stamp of fidelity has replaced the first unfavourable impressions, provided one judges the artist's original painting and not the copies from alien hands, some of which are of indifferent quality.

The first portrait of the reign was equally strangely circumstanced, for it was commissioned not as one might expect by the City of London or one of the leading Commonwealth countries but by a private American citizen. This was the full length by the late Douglas Chandor in the British Embassy in Washington. Mrs. Eleanor Roosevelt had, in fact, suggested the painting, when the Queen was still Princess Elizabeth and was visiting Washington, for presentation to the Embassy and, after her Accession, the Queen decided to continue with the original arrangements. The artist, though born in England, had received his highest recognition and rewards as a fashionable portrait painter in the United States, so that his choice had special emphasis. Douglas Chandor was pruning his peach trees in Texas, in fact, when the letter inviting him to the Palace arrived from London, and he subsequently accomplished the studio background work of the painting in London at the Savoy Hotel. The pose was established at a window of the Yellow Drawing Room in the Palace, overlooking the Mall, and the Queen gave eight sittings of sixty to ninety minutes each. Chandor embarked on every new portrait in an agony of tension, but he happily also found the Queen "a very sympathetic, patient and helpful sitter, showing admirable self-discipline, doing all she could to maintain a difficult momentary pose". To interest his sitters while they rested, Chandor used to work with a mirror behind him, so that he could be watched at work, a gimmicky trick that invariably proved effective. The Queen, he noted, was aware of every false brush stroke. But the Queen is an experienced veteran in the unique relationship of artist and sitter. As a child she was sculptured by Strobl and painted by A. K. Lawrence and Mabel Hankey, as well as De Laszlo. In later girlhood she sat to Sir William Reid Dick.

Between 1945 and 1952 the Queen Mother commissioned paintings and drawings from Rodrigo Moynihan, Saveley Sorina, Edward Halliday, Frederick Whiting, Peter Scott, and Simon Elwes, and the Princess sat in addition to Oswald Birley and Denis Fildes, to Dame Laura Knight — for the Coventry

composite picture — and to Stella Marks for the miniature —
a watercolour on ivory.

Chandor's chief difficulty was his props. The Queen can
sometimes detect a mistaken pose at the outset and tactfully
put it right, but, once a portrait has begun, she never
comments on the likeness. In planning his composition,
Chandor wished to paint the Queen with her youth and
freshness half reflected in a mirror symbolizing the future, but
the oval frame of the mirror turned out to be a monotonous
feature and the console table below it seemed to chop the
picture in half. To break this effect Chandor contrived an
orchid in a Sèvres vase, but the blue had to partner the blue of
the Garter Ribbon, and both became uneven, in the artist's
eyes, in the effect of dusk seen through the windows in the
Mall. Chandor said afterwards that the more he looked at the
painting the more he found things wrong. Yet the world was
satisfied. Curiously enough, another portrait of the Queen at
this time also escaped complete Englishness, for it was
commissioned by H.M.S. *Excellent*, the naval gunnery school,
from Mrs. Irma Hardy, who was Hungarian by birth. In this
case, the Queen could not find the time for a sitting and Mrs.
Hardy worked from the Queen's evening gown, coronet and
jewels on a lay figure. The resulting portrait has a curious
mask-like air.

In her Accession Year the Queen also sat for Margaret
Lindsay Williams, James Gunn, Terence Cuneo, Simon Elwes,
and Denis Fildes. Work had started on some of these
paintings, however, before the Queen came to the Throne, and
Simon Elwes's study of the Garter Installation ceremony had
actually been begun five years before, to be interrupted by the
artist's illness and partial paralysis until he courageously and
slowly learned to paint again with his left hand. Denis Fildes,

who had completed a Princess Elizabeth portrait for the 2nd Battalion the Grenadier Guards, now painted the Queen for the Imperial Defence College. One may count this the first English portrait of the Sovereign and, to date, Fildes has painted seven portraits of the Queen. Yet this is eclipsed by Edward Halliday, who has completed at least twelve portraits from sittings and several others from memory and creative imagination. His patrons have included the Scots Guards, the Cunard Company, the Drapers' Company, the Royal Commonwealth Society, the Sir James Dunn Foundation for a Canadian portrait, and the Maori peoples of New Zealand for a painting now in the Treaty House at Waitangi.

The Queen seldom initiates a portrait herself. One of the rare exceptions was when she invited the Comte Xavier de Poret, a celebrated French equestrian artist, to Windsor in 1958. She wished him to undertake some drawings of Prince Charles and Princess Anne on their ponies, but in the event the Queen also posed on her mare Betsy for two or three further drawings of herself. At the Castle the artist noticed that he was served on a different pattern of china at every meal, a charming touch he thought deliberately intended to please his interest in design. He may or may not have been right. Sir William Hutchison similarly joined the Household at Windsor for a week in 1956 in order that he could see the Queen informally at lunch or when she was relaxing in the evening, thus familiarizing himself with his sitter although the portrait was to be a formal full length in Thistle Robes.

The first portrait for Scotland was, however, completed by Lydia de Burgh for the Argyll and Sutherland Highlanders, and Edward Halliday has since painted the Queen in Garter Robes for the Scots Guards. If other Scottish bodies have proposed sittings without gaining acceptance it is because the Queen obviously cannot assent to every request. After seeing the completion of six portraits in 1956 and four the following year, she felt that a respite would do no harm, and she sat only to Anthony Devas in 1958, to Henry Carr in 1959, and to Norman Hepple and Edward Halliday in 1960. No further portraits were completed until late in 1962. A former Lord Mayor of Manchester openly expressed disappointment that his city had been refused sittings, but the Palace thereupon replied with equal bluntness that it was quite impossible to please everybody. The applicants gaining the Queen's consent have included the Governments of Canada and Australia, the city of Auckland, New Zealand, the city of Hull, the Royal Borough of Windsor, the Royal Naval Barracks at Portsmouth, the United Services Club, Lloyds of London, and the Royal Commercial Travellers' School, as a representative selection. A high proportion of royal portraits has been permitted, on the other hand, to the ancient city companies — the Fishmongers, Goldsmiths, Cutlers, and Drapers. Regiments, too, can and do claim favour from the Queen as Colonel-in-Chief, and portraits have been sponsored by the Grenadier Guards, the Coldstream Guards, Royal Welch Fusiliers, Honourable Artillery Company, Royal Army Ordnance Corps and so forth. But every application for the Queen's time is considered strictly on its merits and an apparent sense of rivalry can be deceptive. The Queen gave sittings to Leonard Boden for the Royal Military Academy, Sandhurst, immediately following the sessions accorded to Denis Fildes for his portrait with Prince Philip for the Royal Naval College, Greenwich, and both these portraits of 1956 had, in fact, been originally and separately proposed three years earlier.

The choice of the artist is left to the proposer and the Palace in practice never recommends a painter. The refusal of sittings is, however, softened by a portfolio of photographs of original portraits of the Queen from which an institution can select an artist to make a copy of an earlier picture, or perhaps an original imaginative work. Thus one of Halliday's 1955 portraits has been copied for the Guildford Chamber of Commerce and a duplicate of the Anthony Devas portrait appears in the Mayor's Parlour in Bolton. Copies of the famous Annigoni portrait, usually by one of his pupils, are always in demand, and two copyists at once have sometimes been at work with their easels in Fishmongers' Hall, where the original picture hangs.

Incidentally, the Duke of Edinburgh's cousin, Queen Helen of Rumania, first brought Annigoni to the notice of the Queen in enthusiastically sending photographs of his paintings from Florence. The Queen herself then ushered Annigoni into the ranks of royal portrait-painters by making her admiration of his work completely obvious. When she paused before his picture of Mrs. Christie Miller at the portrait galleries in Suffolk Street and studied it for some minutes, expressing the hope that he might one day paint her, we know that the wish was persuasive. Thereupon the artist's agents had no difficulty in arranging the contract with the City Guild of the Worshipful Company of Fishmongers for portraits of both the Queen and Prince Philip.

Anthony Devas found the magic sesame when he painted King Faisal of Iraq. Denis Fildes has said candidly that a wide Army acquaintance around his home on Salisbury Plain, fostered by membership of the United Service Club, led to his portrait in Army uniform of King George VI and thus to his commissions for the Queen. Edward Halliday, on the other hand, had specimens of his work submitted with those of other artists for the Drapers' Company portrait in 1949 of the then

Princess Elizabeth, an open competition from which he emerged triumphant.

The rewards of a modern royal portraitist can be considerable, if the artist retains copyright — and his agents usually ensure that he does. Annigoni is reputed to have made £10,000 in two years from magazine and newspaper reproductions, prints, calendars and Christmas cards, and such trifles as the Queen's likeness on Maltese banknotes. A percentage being impossible, Mrs. Mary Gillick received only an inclusive fee, however, for the most widely reproduced portrait of all, the profile head of the Queen, wearing a chaplet of laurel, on the first coins of the reign. The Queen gave portrait sittings both to the artist and to Cecil Thomas, the sculptor who modelled the relief, but Mrs. Gillick was the most self-critical artist of all and no fewer than sixty-three moulds and casts were produced before she was satisfied.

III

Although there have been over twenty portraits of the Queen in evening dress, five in the mantle or robes of an Order of Chivalry and two in uniform, few artists choose to paint the Queen in everyday clothes. The portraitist fears the transience of fashion, and at one time an evening gown of a particularly traditional line was used so often by various artists that the Queen called it her portrait dress. The choice of costume, however, is invariably that of the painter. When a portrait has been authorized an artist is first encouraged to discuss his intentions, the probable pose, the dress and the jewels with one of the Queen's Private Secretaries, or her Press Secretary. After they have assisted him to overcome the initial hurdles of choice, he is then usually taken to the wardrobe rooms on the second floor of the Palace, where the Queen's Dresser will have laid out several evening dresses for the artist's selection and is on hand to provide her expert help in the bewildering choice of jewellery and the decision on whether or not a tiara and the Garter ribbon or other accoutrements will be worn.

At least four artists, namely, James Gunn, Edward Halliday, Annigoni, and Raymond Kanelba, have at times painted the Queen bare-headed. With the Kanelba portrait for the Grenadier Guards, the artist's wish to show the Queen's hair created a difficulty, for the full uniform required the tricorne hat. The point was overcome by showing the Queen in an interior, seated, her tricorne beside her, gloves ready in one hand. The Queen usually approves a painter's preference, and almost as soon as the artist has been ushered to the Yellow Drawing Room or the Balcony Room on the appointed day, Her Majesty appears dressed as he indicated. Initial presentations are quickly over, and the Queen usually comes to subsequent sittings quite alone and takes up the pose required without wasting time. The hour or hour and a half allotted seems always too urgently brief to the artist. Over a series of eight or nine sittings, generally from eleven in the morning until shortly before lunch, every painter, however, experiences the Queen in her varying moods, and thus has the opportunity of discovering that mysterious inner reality without which a likeness fails. Margaret Lindsay Williams once wished to capture a smiling mood and noted the Queen's innate preference for a serious expression. Annigoni at first placed her with her eyes turned away from the window towards the darkest corner of the room. With practised tact, the Queen told him of her delight as a child in looking out of the window at the people and traffic, and thus subtly suggested the pose of thoughtful interest, towards the light, that proved so effective. Sometimes artists find the Queen preoccupied and silent, but more usually she talks gaily over a range of topics: "We talked of everything, ships and sealing wax and cabbages and kings," as Sir Charles Wheeler said. For his three bronzes, the Queen first gave sittings at the Palace and then went to his studio in Cathcart Road, off the Fulham Road in Kensington, taking a tiara in her handbag and posing for seventy-five minutes on each of six occasions. The bare painted brick walls, the clutter of busts, the smell of clay and the rough tables of the studio renewed a familiar atmosphere, for the Queen had also given sittings to Ben Enwonwu, the Nigerian, some years earlier at Sir William Reid-Dick's old studio in St. John's Wood. A sculptor is immobilized by the encumbrances of plaster, wax, stone or wood, with which he must work. An artist can, of course, continue painting at the Palace long after the Queen has left him — not uncommonly he comes back after lunch — and royal visits to artists' studios are comparatively rare. An exception was made for Alfred Thomson, who was a deaf-mute artist, and the Queen went to his Chelsea studio when his painting of Her Majesty's attendance at the Royal Air Force fortieth anniversary banquet was in preparation. Similarly, she sat to Simon Elwes at his studio after his illness, when he was sedulously and painfully learning to paint again with his left hand. Although the Queen's time is limited, however, nothing at the Palace seems to be too much trouble to meet an artist's intentions. When Terence Cuneo painted his occasion picture of the Queen at a Mansion House lunch, a platform was built in one of the more lofty State Apartments in order that he could look down at his sitters as he had done at the Mansion House. Another artist, Leonard Boden, asked if it would be possible to have a lock of the Queen's hair to help in matching his colours, and he duly received it, wrapped in tissue paper, in a little box.

Aside from the Queen's own sittings, a lady-in-waiting occasionally serves as a stand-in, and the Queen has also had a lay figure made to her exact measurements on which an evening gown, robes or uniform can be realistically draped. At the conclusion of a personal sitting, the Queen will sometimes study the portrait, but never directly comments on the likeness, and rarely on the background details. An objection is occasionally overcome by members of her staff, who, ostensibly dropping in afterwards to see how a picture is progressing, sometimes provide a little constructive criticism with such deftness that the artist is unaware of being directed. Miss Lindsay Williams found herself asked whether she had reproduced the colour of the Queen's nails in quite the right shade of pink, and though doubtful at first she agreed afterwards that her mentors were right. Such social niceties are preserved in the case of other royal portraits. When A. K. Lawrence was engaged in portraying Prince Charles and Princess Anne, the Queen and the Queen Mother came in quietly to talk to the children, but neither approached the easel. (The two pastels, however, were highly satisfactory, for they now hang in the Queen's sitting-room.) When Graham Sutherland abandoned his portrait of the Queen Mother — as Augustus John had done twenty years earlier — it was only because of his own dissatisfaction with the preliminary sketches. More cautiously, the Queen herself noted the tiny figures of guardsmen on parade in the background of a Windsor scene by Edward Halliday and pointed out that an officer was doing the duty of a warrant-officer, and at her suggestion a white belt was painted in to denote the figure in rank. Prince Philip, on the other hand, was apt to express his opinions directly and shrewdly.

The Queen is the most practised, as she is the most sought after, sitter in the world; yet when Simon Elwes painted his Royal Naval Barracks portrait, Her Majesty went along to a party at his studio in St. John's Wood to celebrate its completion. Few portraitists of the Queen face their task but with emotion and all are treated with tactful understanding and consideration that goes far beyond duty.

The Queen has never directly commissioned a portrait of herself. The Queen Mother consistently commissioned most of the pictures of her elder daughter as Princess Elizabeth. The Queen in turn enjoyed seeing her own children perpetuated in paint, but usually wished such commissions to be completely private. The well-known series of studies of Princess Anne by the tragically fated Ulrica Forbes were commissioned by Queen Elizabeth the Queen Mother for the choice of a surprise gift to the Queen.

10: THE QUEEN'S GALLERY

I

"The Crown's advisers might show a little more initiative. The Court should give a lead to intelligent patronage of many sorts. For example, it could by its example have made it respectable for every local authority and big company to mind about the quality of its buildings and furnishings. It could have founded a Glyndebourne or continued with more enterprise the tradition of the Royal Picture Collection — or, if these activities don't appeal, promoted other and popular arts, anything so long as the importance of artistic taste was emphasized…" So said Mr. Jo Grimond, M.P., in an article in *Endeavour* in 1961, only seven months before the Queen's Gallery was first opened to the public and when its building was already far advanced. It is a statement with a tattered look, as though torn by the winds of time almost before it could be unfurled: all the stranger and more disquieting for its authorship, even if regarded as a transient *feu d'esprit*. The Crown is above politics (at least, ostensibly so), but if the leader of the Liberal Party and a Privy Councillor knew so little of the Queen or her advisers, what can the man-in-the-street hope to know, confronted as he is with a new literature in which to speak well of the Queen is curiously interpreted as toadying?

Visiting Congress House, the headquarters of the Trades Union Congress, Prince Philip eyed Brian Wall's sculpture and could not resist the impromptu sally, "Is that the Unknown Bricklayer?" His badinage is in context only when we remember that Prince Philip also bought fifteen to twenty modern paintings a year. The Queen Mother, hearing that

181

money was short at Covent Garden Opera House, started a subscription for a row of thirty-five chandeliers to grace the balcony. At another time, forsaking a measure of privacy, she invited members of the Contemporary Art Society to see her pictures at Clarence House. Yet these good deeds won less attention than royal attendance at a steeplechase.

The meaning of the distinction "R.D.I." is known only to the initiated, and successive governments of both major political parties can be blamed if new appointments as Royal Designers for Industry are quietly left to the council of the Royal Society of Arts instead of being incorporated in the Honours List. The distinction was instituted to confer public recognition on designers of high merit; the Queen added the royal prefix, and furniture designers such as Robin Day and the Russells, silversmiths such as David Mellor and R. Y. Goodden, industrial designers like Misha Black, textile designers such as Lucienne Day, artists in ceramics, glass, typography and book-binding are all included in this brotherhood, a little-known academy limited to thirty members. Perhaps if this is to be more celebrated the television cameras should be invoked for a ceremony of installation or an annual assembly with Garter pageantry. Yet the Queen shops at the Crafts Centre whenever possible with as much publicity as the Palace rota systems can obtain; and the Duke of Edinburgh spent hours at his tape-recorder and typewriter preparing the speeches for the Design Centre that seem so outspoken and spontaneous when he delivered them. The Crown can scarcely do more to change the emphasis of public emotion.

We have seen how the Queen and the Duke of Edinburgh continuously acquired works of modern art and consistently worked for artistic purposes. We have watched them bringing imaginative patronage to bear even in the ancient convention-ridden forms of official gifts and presentations. The Queen and her husband have increasingly invited designers, poets, artists and authors to the new cocktail parties, luncheons and dinner-parties that have replaced most of the old formal and outmoded functions at Buckingham Palace; and further they have set an example in adapting the royal residences to modern living which is certainly well known to intelligent architects. We have seen them as if steadily grappling with the illusion that the Crown has no part in the finer intellectual currents of modern life. Now we can only amplify our knowledge if we study the Queen a little closer in her home.

II

From Charles II onwards the domestic taste of a dozen generations is imprinted on the interior of Windsor Castle, and in 1959, as the first major decade of the new Elizabethan reign drew to its close, the Queen and the Duke of Edinburgh called in Sir Hugh and Lady Casson and asked them to prepare schemes for remodelling and furnishing a set of rooms that should be as representative of the best of our time as other suites in the Castle have been of times past. The chosen venue was the King Edward III Tower, where Wyatt had already imposed his tastes on the exterior and the interior was a dark humdrum glomerate of Edwardian guestrooms and clutter. The Queen's instructions were specific: she wished the renovated suite to be an exercise in mid-twentieth-century craftsmanship and design. The furniture and textiles were to be commissioned from prominent living designers or bought from the new ranges of modern manufacturers if they reached the right excellence. Stock patterns could be combined with specially made pieces if they attained the necessary grace, liveliness and high workmanship. The Queen took this experiment in the available elegance of modern living with the seriousness of any housewife. Patterned walls that had become fusty with sixty years of usage were masked with plain panels for her to judge the suitability of plain walls. The Queen and her husband experimented for a time with models and drawings; fabrics and carpets were studied in context, and the Queen even spent an afternoon with a friend in a little interior decoration showroom, leafing through manufacturers' wallpaper pattern books, because she had heard that some good designs were to be found there.

The world has heard all too little of this distinctive contemporary scheme, extending as it did from bedheads and bedside lamps to bathroom plumbing fixtures and even to door furniture. The personal nature of this suite in the Private Apartments detracts a little from the encouragement that the Queen intended. Each piece of furniture was, however, not only wedded to the general scheme but also subject to special scrutiny in its own right. Before all the examples of furnishing passed into royal use, juries of the Furniture Makers' Guild were at Her Majesty's wish invited to examine the pieces, and the Guild Mark was awarded to eighteen of them, an indication to posterity that the Queen's taste in materials and design is shared by her peoples. And for the present, as an editorial of *Design* commented, "the fact that the two topmost people in the land should have commissioned modern architects, artists and designers to do a distinctively contemporary scheme should immensely strengthen the following for the good things of our own day". Queen Ena of Spain remembered these rooms as always unoccupied, the furniture covered by dust-sheets — "dead rooms", as they were known in the family. Revisiting them at the time of the Duke of Kent's wedding, she found that Queen Elizabeth II had restored the sunlight, and chased out the sense of cobwebs and shadows.

The Queen inherited the responsibilities of Windsor Castle after forty years had already been passed under the improving eye of Queen Mary and the discerning taste of Queen Elizabeth the Queen Mother. But Queen Mary had a pervading sense of family associations and ancient tradition, and the Queen Mother's powers as a chatelaine had been curtailed by more than a decade of war and post-war austerity. Threadbare carpets, for example, were patched underneath with canvas. Three great floral carpets first made for Queen Victoria presented a considerable problem even to the resourceful Wilton factory, for the largest looms had long since been dismantled. Visiting a textile exhibition, the Queen stopped at the Wilton stand and, inquired with mock gravity, "And how are *my* carpets getting on?" After no years of usage, the intricately patterned carpet of the White Drawing Room was past useful service. The Queen had stipulated that new carpets should be devised from the Commonwealth, and 38 feet long by 31 feet wide, a replica was woven in one piece in Hong Kong, the canvas backing being woven of Pakistani cotton yarn and Malayan latex, the wool from New Zealand and the United Kingdom. Both at Windsor Castle and Buckingham Palace stocks of silk and damask are kept in store for repairs to sofas, walls and curtains. Lengths of material are laid out to fade in the sun to match up with the old, though the effect is not always successful. Aware that even these replacements are running out, the Queen heard of the remarkable restoration of old fabrics achieved by Lady Meade-Fetherstonhaugh with infusions of the herb saponaria, and went to Uppark to see for herself. According to the upholstery, brocade or material requiring treatment, the infusion is sprayed or brushed on, or the fabric is dipped in it. Flaccid threads regain colour and strength, enabling tears and broken threads to be repaired, and tapestries dating back to Charles II, grospoint armchairs of William and Mary and late eighteenth-century upholstery have been treated with conspicuous success. The Queen enjoys making comparisons and, spending a weekend in Northamptonshire, she visited Kirby Hall, near Gretton, specially to see how this Elizabethan mansion was faring in the hands of the Ministry of Works. Admitted with her party of six on shilling tickets one Saturday afternoon, the Queen was unrecognized.

It says much that the Queen has already secured the impress of her personality upon Windsor Castle and brought it to a higher pitch of perfection both in contemporary comfort and traditional respect. This was particularly apparent when the State Apartments were reopened to the public after the extensive cleaning and redecoration of 1961–2. The stonework of Salvin's Grand Staircase had not been cleaned for almost a century, and the rejuvenation created not an effect of newness but one of care; the fourteenth-century armour became all the more forceful to the imagination by being polished as if urgently ready for wear. The freshly decked walls of the Ballroom, formerly the Van Dyck Room, covered with a new blue silk damask chosen by the Queen, were again a splendid foil to George III's three English crystal chandeliers. In 1962–3, as we have seen, the Queen caused the rooms to revert to their old names so that their history and meaning might be better understood. The Rubens Room was once again the King's Drawing Room: the Picture Gallery resumed its historic place as the Queen's Drawing Room. The Throne Room was placed on view again for the first time in many years. Even the revised guidebook, however, could not profess to be accurate, for pictures listed were liable to be replaced by others. Before these words come to print, the triple portrait of Charles I may be restored to its established position over the Ballroom fireplace. But other paintings may have moved in turn, for the choice of pictures for the Queen's Gallery at Buckingham Palace takes pre-eminence.

III

The future shape of the bombed private chapel at Buckingham Palace had been long under discussion, the plans frequently under revision, before the Queen signified her approval of the basic design by Eric Bedford, chief architect of the Ministry of Works. An exacting client is a challenge to an architect, and the Queen knew precisely what she wanted, even to the pebble-edged flagstones of the new corridor forming the public approach. She wished to retain a private chapel and yet not to waste its space; she desired part of the chapel to be used as an art gallery and yet the whole of the floor area was to be available for worship when an important service required. In this she was unconsciously in step with the young Queen Victoria, who, finding no chapel available when she first took up residence, decided to make one without separation from secular usage.

Queen Victoria allotted space in an octagonal room intended for the display of armour, but had the altar floor and panelled background fixed on castors so that it could be wheeled aside. Unluckily the Queen and Prince Albert could smell the Sunday dinner cooking in the adjacent kitchens as they prayed, and in 1842 Prince Albert suggested that the south conservatory might be converted as a place of worship. John Nash's design of 1831 required little adaptation beyond the walling up of the conservatory windows and the raising of the centre of the roof to admit light by a clerestory supported on cast-iron columns. Badly heated and disproportionately high for its length, the chapel served nearly a hundred years as a focus of Palace worship. Then in September, 1940, on Friday the thirteenth, a stick of six bombs was distributed across the Palace by a German dive-bomber. "The whole thing happened in a matter of seconds. We all wondered why we weren't dead," King George VI recorded in his journal. Two bombs, however, fell without exploding, two exploded in the forecourt, where they raised a ten-foot gusher from a broken water main, the fifth drilled a two-foot hole in the chapel ceiling, and the sixth bomb buried itself harmlessly in the garden. The fifth bomb, exploding, wrecked the chapel and the plumber's shop beneath, where four men were working. Three were injured, though not seriously, and even the material damage was of limited extent. The Gobelins tapestry, for instance, was rescued almost intact from behind the shattered altar, and even Queen Victoria's family Bible, in which all royal births had been recorded, during and since her reign, was retrieved from the debris, dusty but otherwise little harmed. The bomb left the four walls standing, as if tacitly subscribing to a plan, first proposed by a pamphleteer in 1830, that the conservatory, plus corridor space, would make an excellent public art gallery.

The idea lingered, at all events, to strike King George VI with forceful novelty, but the future of the chapel remained unsettled until Ministry of Works architects grew concerned that the walls might be dangerous, and then the Queen and the Duke of Edinburgh seriously proposed the idea of creating a new art gallery. A major objection was that the £45,000 allowance for the repair of war damage would be insufficient. Only £41,000 could be charged to the Royal Palaces Vote, £4,000 was contributed from grant-in-aid funds and the additional cost of the structural alterations, fixtures and fittings, was ultimately borne by the Queen's own private resources.

The ingenuity of the Duke of Edinburgh, can be seen in the quick and successful transformation from private chapel to art gallery and vice versa. In June, 1962, a congregation of over sixty attended the hallowing service of the white and gold chapel, the consecration of the altar, the dedication of the ornaments and chapel furnishings. In mid-July the art critics enjoyed their preliminary view of the first Queen's Gallery exhibition, and strolled admiringly where worshippers had knelt in reverence. Lightweight curtain walls and a stairway have been effectively fixed in position and the lighting enhanced. Yet the Queen's Gallery occupies only one-third of the total chapel area and there is nothing of Queen Victoria's portable altar-floor in the adaptation. The altar occupies its permanent setting at the eastern end, unseen by Gallery visitors. Beneath the balcony at the western end of the reduced chapel, white-painted folding doors can be drawn aside to bring the extended space of the art gallery into use for larger services. The scheme is much as the Queen and Prince Philip foresaw, though necessarily adapted by circumstances. The first announcement of the Queen's plans, for instance, envisaged a gravelled approach path fenced off from the Palace grounds. For increased security, this has become a broad glass-roofed corridor, forty yards long, windowless like the Queen's Gallery itself and affording no view of the gardens. On July 25, 1962, when the Queen's Gallery was first opened, there were the inevitable endurance-test martyrs who waited all night to be first inside. The queue sometimes stretched for half a mile, and some of the 1,610 people who paid their half-crowns on the opening day had never before been in an art gallery. But this was in keeping with the Queen's expressed hope that the exhibition should make a serious contribution to the appreciation of the arts. Rain later in the opening week reduced the crowds. If any visitors were disappointed, it was usually because they had expected to see the State Apartments. But the Gallery has settled down into what the Queen always intended it should be: a contribution to the artistic resources of her capital which, though domestic in scale, sets a notable example to the world.

For the Gallery succeeds in expressing part of the Queen's own personality. For every unimaginative grumbling visitor, there are no doubt ten who enjoy the intimate sense of being admitted to a part of the Queen's private home. This may be due to the flowers from Sandringham and Windsor; the tables and cabinets that stand in accompaniment beneath the pictures; the French clocks and pieces of porcelain that in turn grace the tables. The room is small, and all the more homely by municipal standards, little more than fifty feet broad and long. The eye can take in the splendour of the paintings in a single breathtaking glance as if presented with a microcosm of royal artistic history before turning to closer detail. But this is precisely as the Queen wished. Her Majesty chose the inconspicuous beige rayon canvas that covers the walls, taut-stretched except where it falls in soft curtain folds against the chapel. The polished parquet floor of Burmese teak is a subtle attribute of the Palace atmosphere and the shadowless modern toplighting through a panelled ceiling of translucent squares is unlikely to be improved upon for many years.

At the opening exhibition Sir Anthony Blunt and his colleagues had mounted a representative selection of the Queen's treasures. One's admiration was immediately captured by Vermeer's *The Music Lesson* and Rembrandt's *The Lady With a Fan*. One had but to turn to see Gainsborough's fifteen oval portraits of George III and his family, mounted together, as Gainsborough intended, and beneath this array was the inlaid jewel cabinet "of mahogany and various other woods" that William Vile and John Cobb had made for Queen Charlotte. Turning left to tour the room in detail, one found the early Bellini of a young man, probably from George III's collection; the portrait of Elizabeth I as a princess at which Elizabeth II had gazed when a princess; a Durer portrait from the collection of Charles I and the celebrated triple-head study of the King by Van Dyck from Windsor Castle. Then there was a Claude, Gainsborough's *Duke and Duchess of Cumberland*, Pieter de Hooch's *The Card Players*, and Ter Borch's *The Letter*, in sumptuous proximity with the celebrated Negress Head clock which may have belonged to Marie Antoinette, the silver mirror and table presented to William III, the Holbein of Sir Henry Guildford, Rubens' *Farm at Laeken*, and so much else beyond remembering. It is to be hoped that some of these treasures will again be shown in future exhibitions. One then mounted the stairs to a small collection of Holbein drawings, pencilled sketches from the hands of Michelangelo and Leonardo, a collection of miniatures from the sixteenth and seventeenth centuries. Amid these pleasures one could almost overlook and miss a display case with Fabergé easter eggs and boxes, the Queen's Garter jewel, and the diadem of pearls and diamonds which she is seen wearing in her postage-stamp portraits.

This was only the first of the many exhibitions that will in future allow the royal works of art to be more widely seen. Later exhibitions will develop certain themes in the Royal Collection and its history, perhaps framing a specialized view of the Primitives or the Dutch and Flemish pictures, perhaps devising a theme on the rich and varied Canalettos or placing a special emphasis on the moderns.

IV

The Queen has had her way. Precisely two hundred years after George III bought Buckingham House, Queen Elizabeth II as his direct descendant through six generations has returned the enjoyment of some part of its pleasures to the nation. The Queen was born into the cultivated aesthetic appreciations of a select and small segment of society, and in the course of her maturity she has placed not least among her acts of national leadership the encouragement and a wider understanding of the arts, and thus a wiser use of leisure. The extension of privilege, not its lessening, sees a notable relaxation, not a lowering, of the barriers. A crossing-sweeper plying his trade outside the gates of the Palace could not have dreamed of entering its precincts nor conceived the thought of enjoying its works of art with enlightened pleasure. This facility is perhaps part of the democratization of monarchy, but the Queen has made it possible, and in sharing her pleasures and making this a direct and honourable gesture to her people, she has assuredly disarmed many of the opinionated but not powerful critics of the Throne.

We began this book with the record of an earlier gesture, involving the approval and direct patronage of the contemporary artist. We have studied the influences that formed, nourished and extended the Queen's constantly improving taste to a standpoint of personal interest where, in the phrase of a distinguished contemporary, it is "vivid, informed and conspicuously effective". If, unfashionably, we have found more to praise than to criticize, it is not a failing. We have ascertained that far from knowing or caring little of

192

art, the Queen practises a personal and deliberate involvement, with vital discernment and the conviction of love. There are signs enough that the fine arts may be raised among the finest jewels symbolized in her crown. The Queen long since acquired discipline and dedication. It is only now that the future shape and strength of her dedication begins to be seen.

APPENDIX: THE PORTRAITS OF H.M. QUEEN ELIZABETH II

A checklist in chronological order, dated from completion.

1. 1952. Painted by Margaret Lindsay Williams. A ¾ length, seated, in evening dress with tiara and Garter ribbon. Owned by the artist. (Painted for reproduction.)
2. 1952. By Douglas Chandor. A full length, standing, in evening dress with tiara and Garter ribbon. Owned by the British Embassy, Washington. (Commissioned by Mrs. Eleanor Roosevelt.)
3. 1952. By Mrs. Hardy. No sitting given, but evening dress and jewels lent. Owned by H.M.S. *Excellent*, Whale Island.
4. 1952. By Denis Fildes. A ¾ length, seated in evening dress with diadem and Garter ribbon. Owned by the Imperial Defence College. (Also copied.)
5. 1952. By Terence Cuneo. The Queen laying foundation stone of new building of Lloyds. Owned by Lloyds.
6. 1953. By James Gunn. A full length, standing, in white fur, evening dress, diadem and Garter ribbon. Owned by Royal Regiment of Artillery.
7. 1953. By Terence Cuneo. A painting of the Coronation ceremony, commissioned by the Queen's Lieutenants. Owned by H.M. The Queen.
8. 1954. By James Gunn. THE STATE PORTRAIT. Coronation robes with Regalia, wearing diadem.
9. 1954. By Denis Fildes. A full length, seated, in evening dress, with tiara and Garter ribbon. Owned by Royal Army Ordnance Corps. (Also copied.)

10. 1954. By Denis Fildes. A full length, seated, in evening dress, with tiara and Garter ribbon. Owned by United Services Club. (Also copied.)

11. 1954. By W. A. Dargie. A ¾ length, seated, "mimosa" evening dress, tiara but no Garter ribbon. Owned by the Government of Australia.

12. 1955. By Simon Elwes. A full length, standing, in evening dress, with diadem and Garter ribbon. Owned by Royal Naval Barracks, Portsmouth.

13. 1955. By Pietro Annigoni. A ¾ length, standing, in Garter robes, with no hat. Owned by Fishmongers' Company.

14. 1955. By Denis Fildes. A full length, seated, in evening dress, with tiara and Garter ribbon. (A version of R.A.O.C. portrait. One sitting given.) Owned by the Guildhall, Windsor.

15. 1955. By Terence Cuneo. The Queen drinking from the Queen's Cup at Mansion House Lunch. Owned by Goldsmiths' Company.

16. 1955. By Edward Halliday. A ¾ length, seated, in evening dress, with Garter ribbon and tiara. (A sketch for portrait for Royal Commercial Travellers' School.) (Also copied.)

17. 1955. By Edward Halliday. Full length, seated in evening dress, with Garter ribbon and tiara. Owned by Royal Commercial Travellers' School. (Also copied.)

18. 1955. By Edward Halliday. A ¾ length, seated, in evening dress, with Garter ribbon and tiara. Globe in background. Owned by Treaty House, Waitangi, New Zealand.

19. 1955. By Raymond Kanelba. A ¾ length, seated, in Grenadier tunic, riding habit, hat shown but not worn. Owned by Grenadier Guards.

20. 1956. By Edward Seago. Full length in Coldstream uniform, mounted on police horse Winston. Owned by

Coldstream Guards.

21. 1956. By Lydia de Burgh. A ¾ length, seated, in evening dress, no tiara or Garter ribbon. Owned by Argyll and Sutherland Highlanders.

22. 1956. By A. C. Davidson-Houston. A ¾ length, seated, in evening dress, with Garter ribbon and tiara. Owned by Royal Welch Fusiliers.

23. 1956. By Edward Halliday. Full length, standing, in evening dress, with Garter ribbon and tiara. Owned by War Memorial Museum, Auckland. (Also copied.)

24. 1956. By Sir William Hutchison. Full length, standing, in Thistle robe, with Victorian Order ribbon and tiara. Owned by Company of Merchants of City of Edinburgh.

25. 1956. By Denis Fildes. Full length, seated, with Prince Philip standing. The Queen in evening dress with Garter ribbon and tiara. Prince Philip in naval uniform. Owned by Royal Naval College, Greenwich.

26. 1957. By Leonard Boden. A ¾ length, seated, in red Bath robe and tiara. Owned by Royal Military Academy, Sandhurst.

27. 1957. By Terence Cuneo. The Queen departing from Hull by Royal Barge for State visit to Denmark. Owned by City Corporation of Hull.

28. 1957. By Mrs. L. Newton. A ¾ length, seated, in evening dress, with Garter ribbon and diadem. Owned by Government House, Ottawa.

29. 1957. By Denis Fildes. Full length, seated, in evening dress with Garter ribbon and tiara. (A version of R.A.O.C. portrait. One sitting given.) Owned by Cutlers' Company.

30. 1958. By Anthony Devas. Full length, standing, in evening dress, with Garter ribbon and tiara. Owned by Honourable Artillery Company.

31. 1959. By Henry Carr. Full length, seated, in evening dress. Owned by the Air Council.
32. 1960. By Norman Hepple. In Bath mantle. Owned by Bomber Command.
33. 1960. By Edward Halliday. In Garter robes. Owned by Scots Guards.

No further portraits completed until autumn, 1962.

A NOTE TO THE READER

If you have enjoyed this book enough to leave a review on **Amazon** and **Goodreads**, then we would be truly grateful.

The Estate of Helen Cathcart

Sapere Books is an exciting new publisher of brilliant fiction and popular history.

To find out more about our latest releases and our monthly bargain books visit our website: **saperebooks.com**

www.ingramcontent.com/pod-product-compliance
Lightning Source LLC
Chambersburg PA
CBHW051514030726

47592CB00006B/2266